Sculpting the
FEMALE FACE
& FIGURE IN WOOD

Sculpting the
FEMALE FACE
& FIGURE IN WOOD

A Reference and Techniques Manual

IAN NORBURY

FOX CHAPEL
PUBLISHING

ISBN 978-1-56523-742-1

Library of Congress Cataloging-in-Publication Data

Norbury, Ian.
 Sculpting the female face & figure in wood / Ian Norbury.
      p. cm.
 Includes index.
 ISBN 978-1-56523-742-1
 1. Wood-carving--Technique. 2. Wood-carved figurines. 3. Women in art. 4. Face in art. I. Title.
 TT199.7.N683 2012
 736'.4--dc23
                            2012013993

To learn more about the other great books from Fox Chapel Publishing, or to find a retailer near you, call toll-free 800-457-9112 or visit us at *www.FoxChapelPublishing.com*.

Note to Authors: We are always looking for talented authors to write new books. Please send a brief letter describing your idea to Acquisition Editor, 1970 Broad Street, East Petersburg, PA 17520.

Printed in China
First printing

DEDICATION

This book is dedicated to women everywhere—they are all beautiful. As I grow older, I am surrounded by more beautiful women—my daughter Jayne, my daughter-in-law Ruth, my four grandchildren Katherine, Jennifer, Julia, and Chloe and my beautiful wife, Betty, my greatest inspiration.

ACKNOWLEDGMENTS

I would like to thank Keith Cooper for the use of his photographic skills and Donna, Nathaly, and Julia for sharing their beauty. Also, my thanks to Mr. and Mrs. Timothy Whitney, Mr. and Mrs. Stanley Golding, Mr. and Mrs. Paul Falca, Mr. and Mrs. Simon Channing Williams, Mr. Martin Brown, and Mr. and Mrs. Hamish Bradwell for permitting their sculptures to be illustrated. Finally my thanks to Sharon Valenzuela for translating my appalling handwriting into type and the team at Fox Chapel for producing the book.

Table of Contents

About the Author

Ian Norbury was born in Sheffield, England in 1948 and educated in Hampshire. After selling his first picture at the age of 15 and being dismissed from the woodwork class he began his career as an artist, selling pictures from local galleries until he went to Cyprus in 1965. He worked in Cyprus for six years painting portraits, landscapes and decorating nightclubs until 1971 when he returned to the United Kingdom to marry Betty. He continued painting, mainly racehorses, until 1975 when he went to St Paul's College, Cheltenham, to study art education. Here he continued to develop his growing interest in three-dimensional art, particularly woodcarving. When he graduated in 1980 he set up a woodcarving studio in an old bakery near the center of Cheltenham.

Ian rose rapidly through the ranks of British woodcarvers, having a solo exhibition every year, regularly contributing to magazines, and writing his first book *Techniques of Creative Woodcarving* in 1983. This book is still in print in three languages and sold worldwide.

Several more books followed as well as seminars and workshops in Switzerland, Iceland, Australia, New Zealand, Ireland, Canada, and America. Ian's two three-month tours of the United States have covered many major cities, and his ability as a teacher has created a huge demand for his services. He was the first woodcarver to produce teaching CDs. These are in his own inimitable style, and as one student put it, "…it is like standing at the great man's shoulder while he works."

Ian's ability as a wood sculptor is based on his skilled draftsmanship and a pragmatic technical approach, which gets the job done as efficiently as possible regardless of method. His innovative techniques are matched by his original and imaginative subjects, which have given him financial success and an enviable reputation among art lovers in Britain.

Much of his work is based on European folklore and mythology combined with cynical tongue-in-cheek sideswipes at the pomposity of contemporary life. This finds an easy rapport with audiences. His great technical expertise in the rendering of detail and his acute observations of expressions and appearances are irresistible to many people. In recent years his innovative use of mixed timbers, inlays of colored woods, metals, stones, shells and gems, have given his work new impetus. Of course he is equally known for his exquisitely made nude figures and portrait busts, which are the usual subjects of his teaching seminars.

Ian now lives with his wife Betty in the Republic of Ireland, but still maintains a house, studio, and gallery in England.

Introduction

by IAN NORBURY

Some of the earliest prehistoric artifacts to have been found are representations of the female form and this fashion has continued unabated throughout history. The shape these sculptures have taken ranges from the painstakingly realistic imitation to the impenetrable abstractions of contemporary art. Most of these artists were, I believe, attempting to create an ideal body. We woodcarvers, in our humble efforts, are doing exactly that but perhaps lack the skill to do so.

In this book, I have tried to set down a systematic approach to creating the basic female torso and head. Using this system as a starting point the reader can adapt the shape to conform with his/her personal vision of female beauty.

I would emphasise that very careful measurement is crucial to success, particularly in the face. The human body is remarkably symmetrical, although older faces do tend to become less so, and although there is an infinite variety of bone structure, muscle development, and fat distribution, the two halves are always the same.

I nearly always use limewood (the U.S. equivalent is basswood) for females because I think the finely sanded appearance of these woods are the most appropriate. Also they are very easy to carve and readily available.

These projects have been successfully completed by many hundreds of my students and I am confident that by carefully following the instructions you can do the same and progress to carvings of your own design.

—Ian

The Four Seasons

Left to right: Spring, Summer, Autumn (Fall) and Winter.

In these carvings, I have translated the traditional theme of the cycle of the seasons into womanhood. Spring is a young girl, shy and not fully developed. Summer is fully mature, vigorous and aware of her own body. Autumn is placid, ripe and content, while Winter is sadder and beginning to fade. Each torso was carved from pitch pine in 1986 and is somewhat stylized.

Each figure: 18" x 5" x 5" including plinth

Walnut Torso

This exuberant figure is carved from a large block of beautiful walnut.

30" high

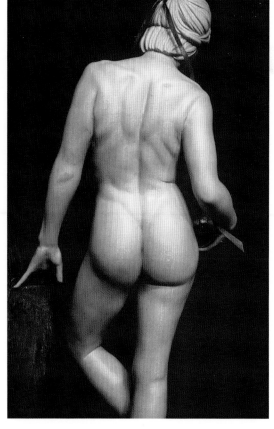

Bronze Torso

This bronze started out as a woodcarving that I then copied in plaster and had cast in bronze. This figure is my only excursion into that medium, which I found a very tedious and disappointing process.

Detail of Atalanta

This figure shows the effect of copying a live model exactly as seen, resulting in a rather homely looking woman, but not really what one expects in a sculptured nude.

15" high

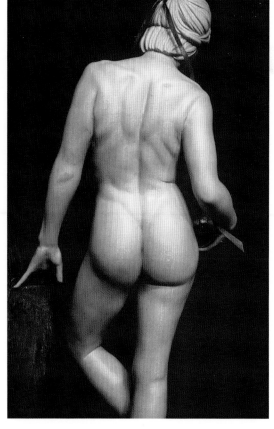

CHAPTER 1

Taking Photographs & Producing Drawings

SECTION 1:
The Female Face

Taking good photographs is an important part of carving the female face. The more accurately you take your photographs, the easier it will be to produce working drawings and carvings of the subject's head. For our purposes in this book, I have found that photographs are infinitely more useful than anatomical drawings that show the underlying muscle structure of the face; therefore, this chapter will focus on using photographs as reference material.

Ideally the subject should be looking directly at the camera. Check this by observing whether both ears are equally visible. Because you are photographing a living subject, her pose may have moved between checking the position of the ears and pressing the shutter; and so, the process must start again. The side view is easier to photograph, but the head must be held at the same angle as in the front-view photograph. (See **Figures 1** and **2**.) Failure to observe these rules can create problems in the pattern-making process.

The same rule of thumb holds true when you are photographing a woman's head that is turned on her shoulders. In this case, it is still easier to photograph her head from the front, as she looks directly at the camera, rather than to photograph her shoulders from the front. (**See Figure 3**.) The photographs taken at A and B will produce perfect pictures. The photograph taken at C will produce an image that is more difficult to work from. Position D shows how to correctly photograph a figure with her head turned.

Taking photographs too close to your subject will produce distorted pictures that show big noses and small ears. This effect will vary more or less from camera to camera. The further away you take your photographs and the longer the lens you use, the more accurate your photographs will be.

Ideally, you should take photographs of your subject from the front, the back, both sides, and the four corners in between. Also take photographs of the subject looking up and looking down. Finally, take a few detail

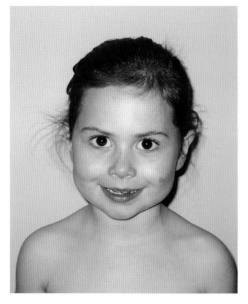 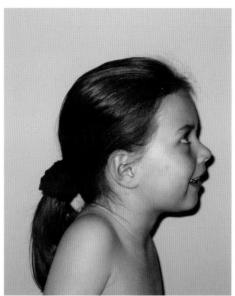

Figure 1:

The front view and side view photographs must show the subject in alignment. Notice in the front view photo how Julia is looking directly at the camera, while in the side view photo she is looking up. The difference in alignments will make pattern-making difficult.

Figure 2:

Here the model, Donna, is looking directly at the camera in the front view, and she maintains that head alignment for the side view. Pattern making in this case will be made easier due to the correct alignment of the head in both photographs.

 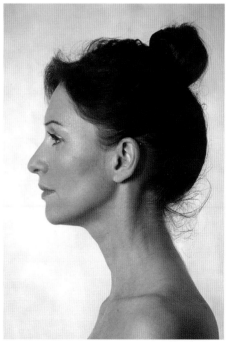

Sculpting the Female Face & Figure in Wood   **13**

shots. Detail shots are invaluable and will aid you in the drawing and carving process. (**See Figure 4**.)

Obtain prints of the photographs and make sure the front and side views are exactly equal in size. This can be done on a photocopier or with a computer. On a photocopier, make an enlarged copy of the front view so that the face is about six inches high. Then measure very carefully the distance between the lower edge of the eye and the joining of the lips on the photocopy. Take the same measurement from the side view photograph. The measurement from the photocopy divided by that from the photograph is the multiplying factor required to enlarge or reduce the photograph to make it equal to the copy. (**See Figure 5**.)

Check that the two photocopies are really the same size; then, trace the outlines and the main features of the front view and one side view. Reverse these tracings to get the back view and the second side view. Reversing the tracings ensures that the four views are identical in outline. Of course, some features, such as the hair on the model in Figure 2, may differ from side to side. Those differences will need to be incorporated by tracing them into the reversed drawings.

When you have produced four tracings, affix them to a drawing board and check that all the main features line up. (**See Figure 6**.) Some features are more important than others in this stage of the process. The hair, ears and neck are not crucial; but, any large discrepancy in the two main views between the levels of the eyes, the nose, the mouth and the chin will cause considerable problems when it is time to begin the carving process.

When you are satisfied that the front and side profiles are correct, the tracings can be enlarged or reduced to fit the wood block you are using.

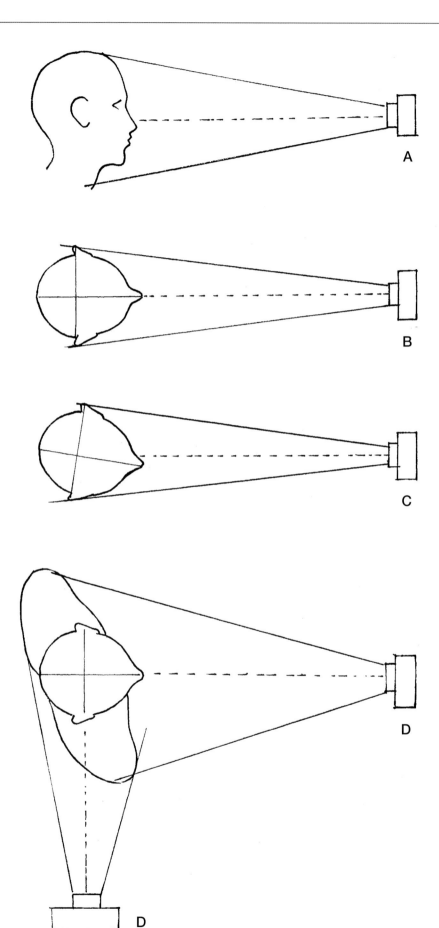

Figure 3:

Finding the proper camera angle is essential to taking good photographs of your subject. Positions A and B are ideal for a subject whose face and shoulders are facing the camera straight on. Position D is ideal for a subject whose face, but not shoulders, is facing the camera. Position C should be avoided.

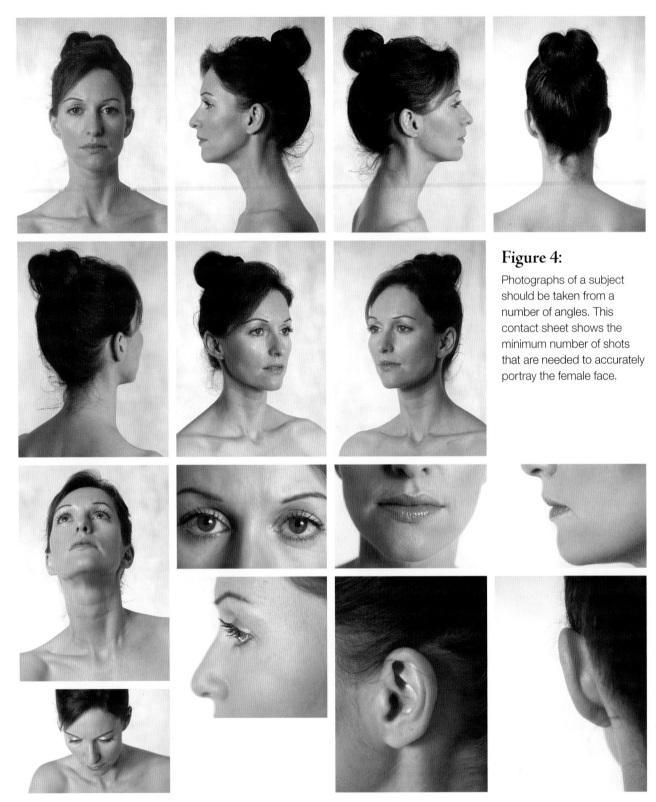

Figure 4:

Photographs of a subject should be taken from a number of angles. This contact sheet shows the minimum number of shots that are needed to accurately portray the female face.

Photocopy

Photograph

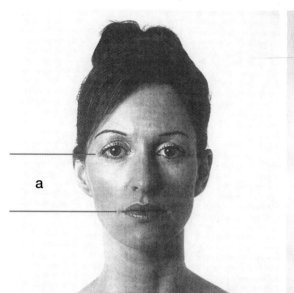

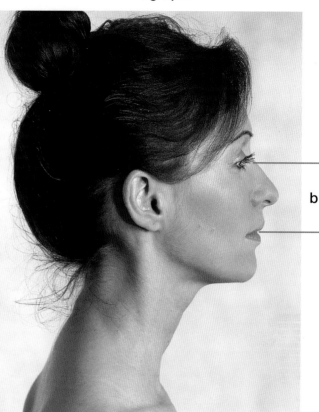

a

b

Figure 5:

All of the photographs of your subject must be
enlarged or reduced to the same height before
you begin to create your pattern. Use the formula
below to make sure the front, side and back views
are the same height.

PHOTOCOPY HEIGHT	÷	PHOTOGRAPH HEIGHT	=	MULTIPLYING FACTOR TO ENLARGE/REDUCE PHOTOGRAPH
(a)		(b)		(c)
12 mm	÷	16 mm	=	0.75%

Figure 6:

When the photographs are the same size, trace the outlines and the main features. Be sure that
the eyes, nose, lips and chin line up correctly from tracing to tracing.

SECTION 2:

The Female Figure

The lady in the photographs is a professional model who has tried her best to adopt an identical pose for eight separate pictures. This is virtually impossible and inevitably there will be variations in the different views.

TAKING PHOTOGRAPHS

Taking photographs of a live model for carving is quite difficult. If the camera is at waist height, it is looking up at the model's head and down at her feet.

Look carefully at **Figure 1**. Here you will see that the right elbow is level with the forehead and the left elbow is level with the top of the head. Now look at **Figure 2**. You will see that the right elbow is level with the top of the head and the left elbow is level with the forehead. The positions are reversed.

Bear in mind always that a nude, unless it is a portrait of an individual, is not a reproduction of a person with his or her clothes off. A nude is the creation of the artist. The model is a guide, not a blueprint.

Now study **Figure 3** and **Figure 4**. In Figure 3, it is clear that the model is standing on a flat, horizontal surface. In Figure 4, the far foot appears higher than the nearer one, even though the model is still standing on the same flat, horizontal surface.

All of this is very obvious, but clearly the pictures cannot be used as they are for the basis of working drawings. Some redrawing is necessary.

Figure 1

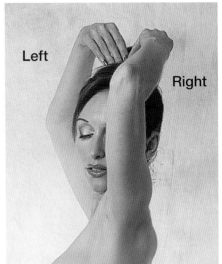

Figure 2

In comparing these two photographs, you will notice that the positions of the elbows are reversed. In Figure 1 the right elbow is level with the forehead and the left elbow is level with the top of the head. In Figure 2 the right elbow is level with the top of the head and the left elbow is level with the forehead.

These effects, which are worse on some camera lenses than others, can be reduced by using a longer lens and moving farther and farther away from the model. Thus, from a distance of 30 feet the pictures would be far more accurate. An even better method than this one is to take a series of photographs at floor, hip, shoulder and eye levels. From eight positions—front, back, both sides and the four points between—this makes a total of 32 photographs. The front, back and side views are obviously most important. The point: If you have a model and a camera you are very lucky, so make the most of it.

> **Note:** The words "left" and "right," when used throughout the demonstration that follows, always refer to left and right as seen on the figure from the front. Therefore, what appears to be the left side when looking at a photo of the back of the carving is still referred to as the right side.

MAKING PLANS

The problems set out previously are not so great on a torso because the extremes of the figure are not being used, but some judgment is still required to make accurate plans.

Clearly, the front view gives a fairly accurate representation of the dynamics of the figure; therefore, this pose is used as the basic position.

To begin making plans, first make a photocopied enlargement of the front view. Then by very accurate measurement of the height of the figure in the front and side photographs, enlarge the side view to exactly the same size as the front view. (**See Figure 5.**) Trace the outlines of the model.

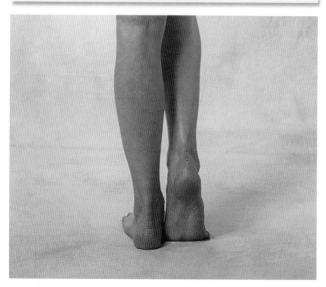

Figure 3

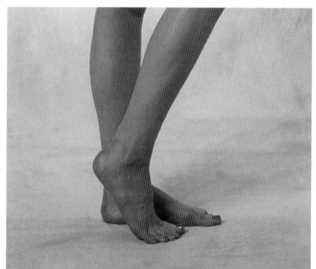

Figure 4

Camera angles and lenses can affect how an image appears on film. In Figure 3 it is clear that the model is standing on a level floor. In Figure 4 the model is still standing on the same level floor, but her feet appear to be on different planes.

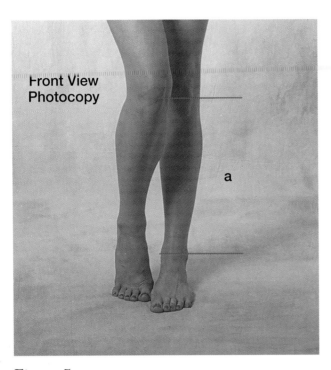

**Front View
Photocopy**

a

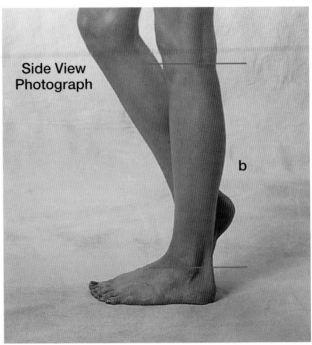

**Side View
Photograph**

b

Figure 5:

Photocopy and enlarge the front view to the desired size. Measure the height of the photocopy and use the formula below to figure out how much to enlarge or reduce the side view.

PHOTOCOPY HEIGHT	÷	PHOTOGRAPH HEIGHT TO ENLARGE/REDUCE PHOTOGRAPH	=	MULTIPLYING FACTOR
(a)		(b)		(c)
41 mm	÷	54 mm	=	0.75%

Fix the two photocopies on a drawing board precisely level at a certain point—the bottom of the breast, for example. (**See Figure 6, Line A.**) Now, from significant points on the front view, rule horizontal lines across to the side view. (**See Figure 6, Lines B–I.**) This exercise will show you where the points on the side view should actually be and how to position the pictures accordingly.

Looking at the drawing, you can see that the lower edge of the right breast and an estimated line of the true floor surface are both level. However, the feet are clearly wrong and the left knee is too low on the front view. The arms are also very inaccurate on the side view.

In the revised details the arms, feet and knees have been redrawn to make both views coincide. (See Figure 6, red illustrations.)

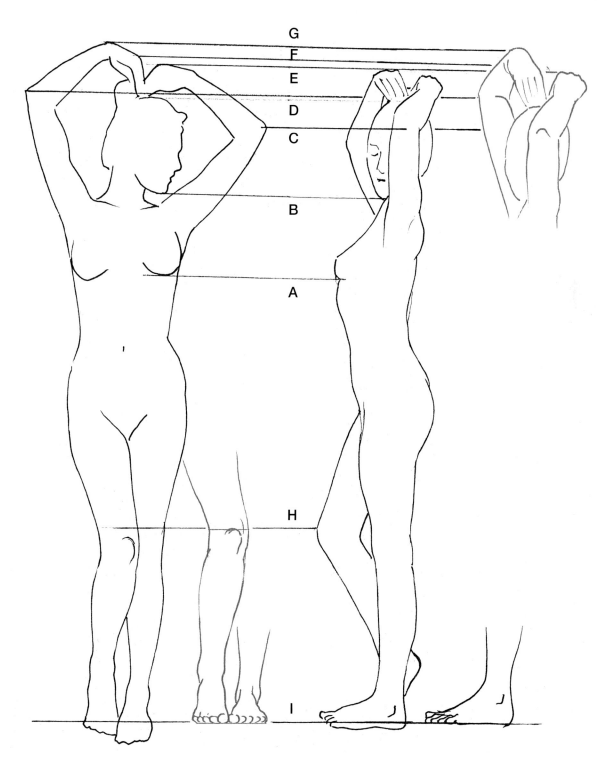

Figure 6:

This figure shows outlines traced from the enlarged photocopies. Line A is used to align the two plans correctly. Notice that the feet, the left knee and the arms on the side view are not in alignment. The red illustrations show the corrections that need to be made to reconcile the two outlines.

CREATING DRAWINGS

My next step is to create drawings from the patterns and the photographs. In these drawings I attempt to rationalize the surface forms of the figure into more clearly defined areas. (**See Figures 7, 8, 9 and 10.**) These illustrations are not anatomical drawings, but more indicators of what to look for in the photographs.

As you'll notice, some of the shapes are not discernable on the photographs of the model. It would take a book full of pictures using different light sources to bring out all the shapes on the body. These drawings help to define those shapes.

The final step is to create patterns based on the photographs, the plans and the drawings. You'll find the patterns for this model in the next chapter where I'll also show you how to carve this piece.

THE ANATOMY DIAGRAMS

Knowledge of anatomy would be a wonderful asset for any figure carver. I have studied anatomy for twenty years, and it is still a problem. People vary so much—different body proportions, different muscular development, different fat deposits—all of which tends to make nonsense of anatomy diagrams. Most anatomy drawings seem to be uniformly based on male bodybuilders, showing sharply defined muscles where ordinary people have empty, sagging skin. Furthermore, many of the surface muscles shown in the diagrams are only thin sheets that actually reveal the structures underneath.

However, a good book on anatomy—used as a diagrammatic basis from which to work, and which can then be adjusted to your own ideals—is probably the easiest way to work and is the method I use. I recommend *Human Anatomy for Artists* by Eliot Goldfinger as the most comprehensive book I have found to date.

Of course, the ideal solution when you do not understand a part of anatomy is to look at a real, live person. For the purposes of this book, I have included photographs of a live model at the beginning of each demonstration and anatomy sketches throughout the demonstrations as relevant to carving that particular part of the torso.

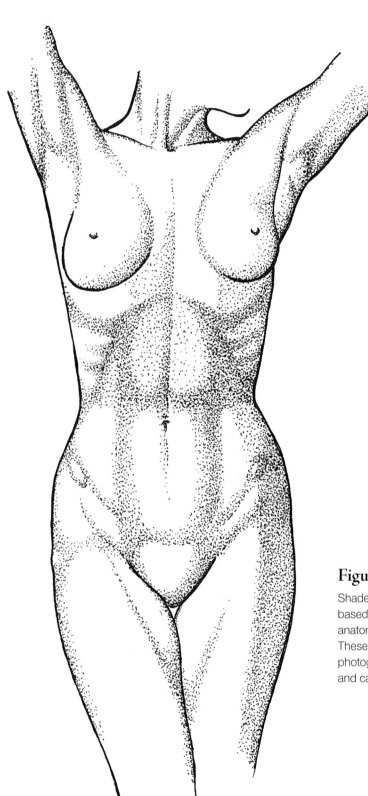

Figure 7:

Shaded drawings of the outlines, based on the photographs and some anatomical knowledge, show more detail. These details are not always obvious on photographs due to lighting conditions and camera position.

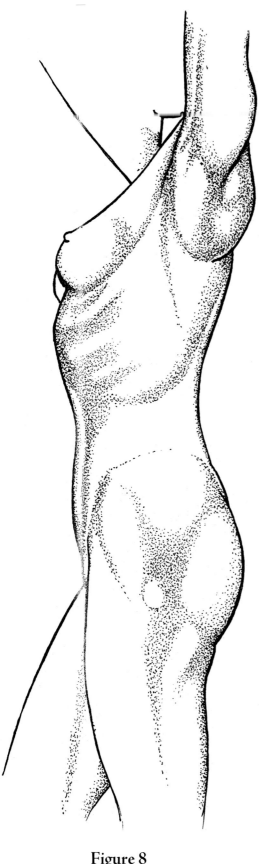

Figure 8

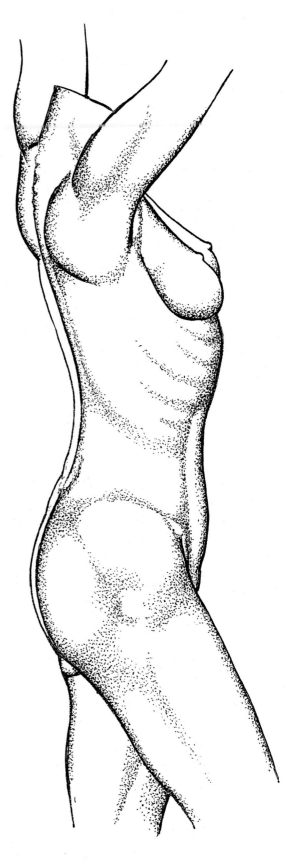

Figure 9

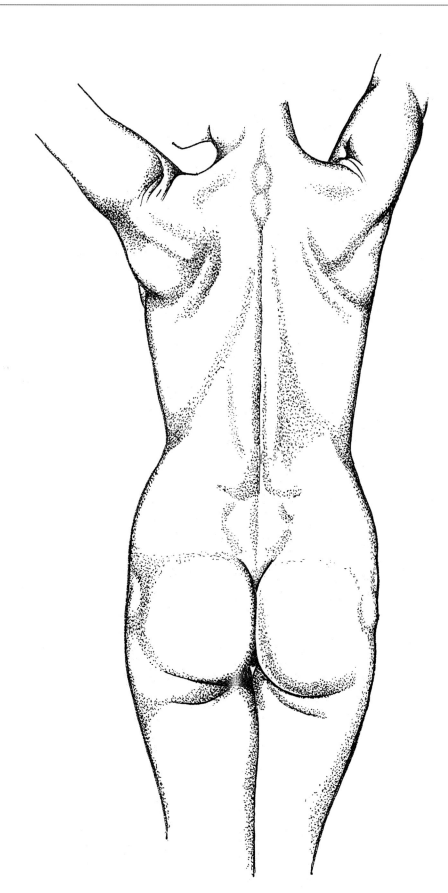

Figure 10

CHAPTER 2

Carving a Classic European Woman's Face

The model for this project is a typical white northern European woman. Donna is a professional model who has very little body fat and a rather angular face with few lines. Despite her leanness, there is very little visual evidence of the anatomy of the face. This is due to the fact, as I mentioned earlier, that many of the differences among women's faces are the results of bone structure and fat deposits, not the muscles that support the face.

TOOL CHOICE

The tools that can be used to carve this face are many and varied. Long experience has shown me that many of my students will make do with the tools they have and are not likely to buy a new set of gouges to carry out one project. Furthermore they may be working on a very different scale, making any tool list I could provide irrelevant. For this reasons, I have not provided a tool list for this project. Whatever tools you choose to use, keep them very sharp.

I will recommend highly that you have one tool on hand: a pair of finely pointed dividers. Measuring the drawings and transferring these measurements to the wood accurately is vitally important, and you must bear in mind that a size on a flat drawing cannot be transferred onto a curved surface without some degree of error.

GATHERING REFERENCE MATERIAL

The fifteen photographs on the following pages are about as near to having a live model as you can get. Study all the views of the head at all times, comparing the lines of the profiles with the shapes you are making in the wood. It is all too easy to carve a front view and a side view that both look good, but the in-between views are all wrong.

Remember you are working in three dimensions, not two, so you must check your work from above and below as well. Many times I have taught students who only look at the wood and forget the photographs and the drawings. There are no answers in the wood.

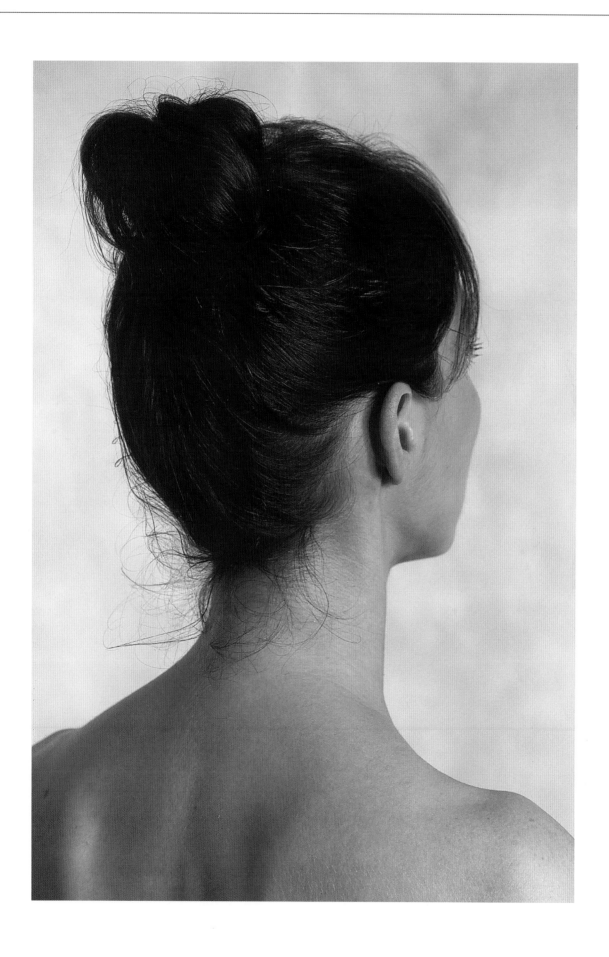

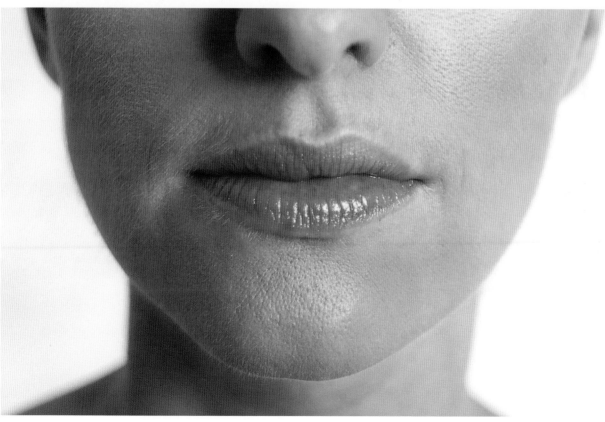

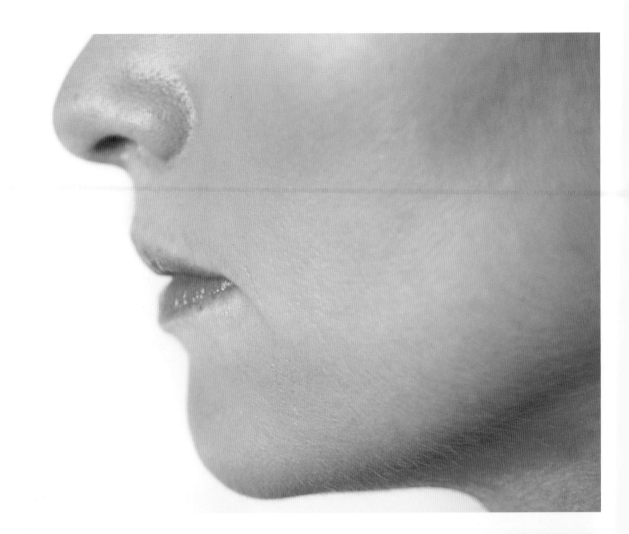

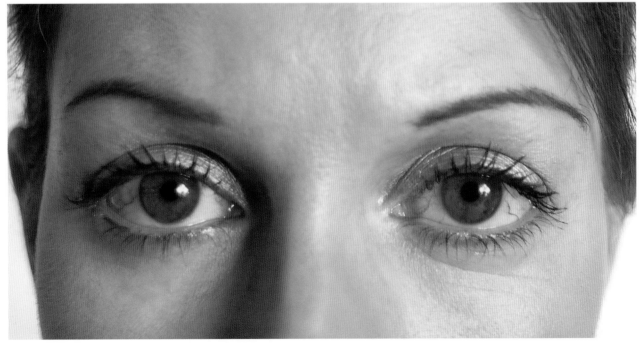

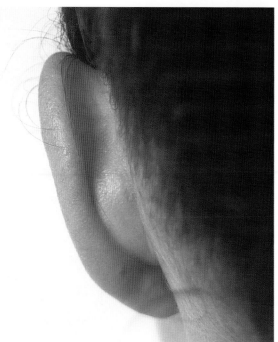

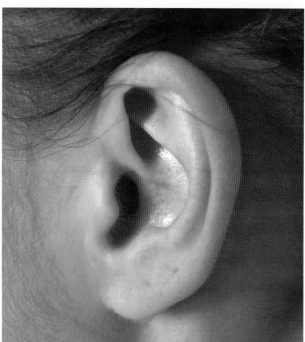

FACE PATTERN: CLASSIC EUROPEAN WOMAN

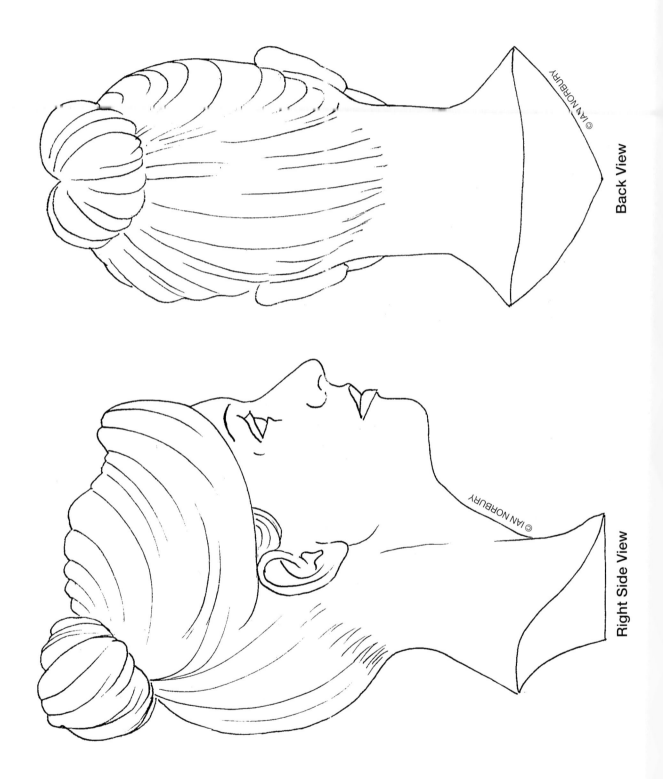

Back View

Right Side View

FACE PATTERN: CLASSIC EUROPEAN WOMAN

© IAN NORBURY

Left Side View

© IAN NORBURY

Front View

Carve the Head to Shape

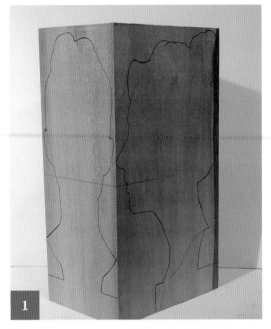

1

Plane the block of wood (5½" x 8" x 13") perfectly square on all sides. Trace the front drawing and right side patterns (pages 38 and 39) on two adjacent sides of the block. Use the base and the lips as datum lines to ensure that the two drawings are perfectly level.

2

Check that the bandsaw table is set absolutely square to the blade. Then bandsaw the front view. Notice that the cut is as close to the line as possible, ensuring that the dimensions of the sawn blank are identical to the drawings. Always follow the manufacturer's instructions regarding safety.

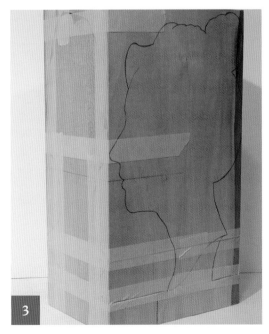

3

Use masking tape to secure the two main pieces of waste wood in place. You are now ready to make the second cut.

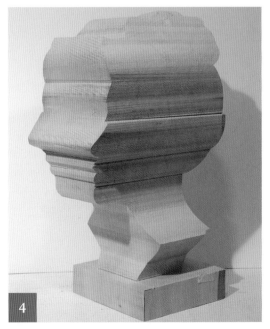

4

The bandsawing is complete and the carving is ready to be mounted on a vice or clamp.

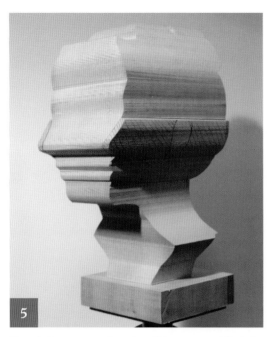

The obvious areas of waste will be removed first. As much of the shaping as possible will be done while the head is still square and easier to measure. First, locate the ears by measuring from the front and the back of the head. The top and the bottom of the ears are marked by bandsaw cuts.

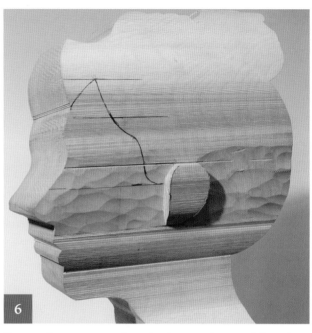

Remove the waste wood, cutting in squarely around the ears. Now, by measurement from the front profile, mark the hairline.

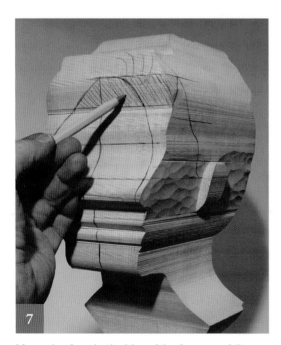

Measuring from both sides of the face, carefully mark in the centerline; then, measuring from the centerline out, draw in the outline of the face, equal on both sides. A large triangular wedge of wood needs to be removed from the forehead.

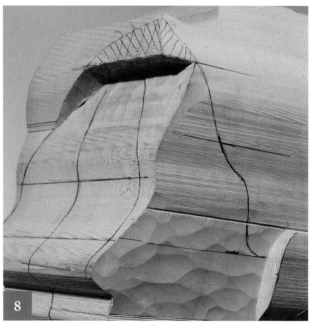

This area has been removed. A second triangular block needs to be removed to complete the line of the coif of the hair.

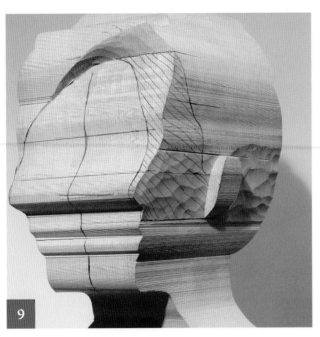

9

The triangular piece has been cut away, following the curved shape of the hair. Mark the wood to be removed between the line of the face and the hair.

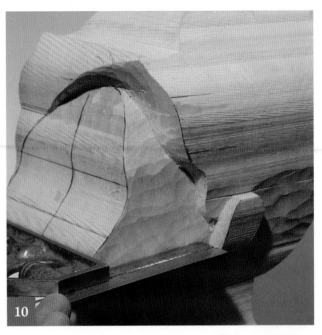

10

The waste wood has been cut away. Notice how the hairline recedes from the surface of the face at a perfect 90-degree angle. The two sides of the face must be parallel or distortion will appear later in the carving.

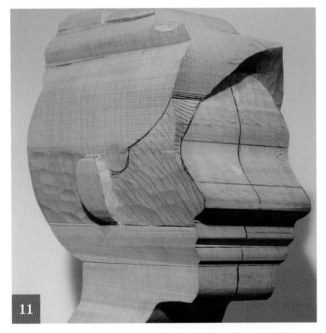

11

Repeat this operation on the opposite side of the face. Check that the two sides are parallel, not tapering outward or inward.

12

The two corners on both sides of the chin can now be removed.

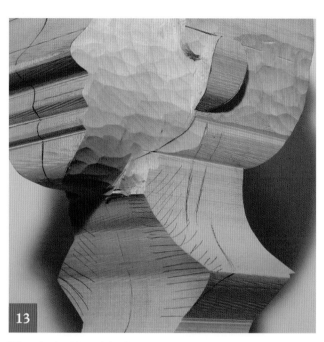

When both sides of the face have been blocked in, mark the two corners on both sides of the throat to be rounded back.

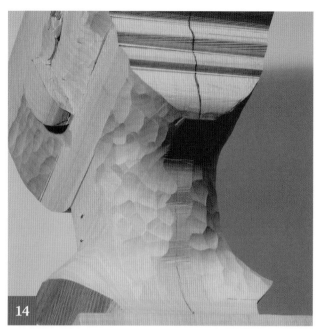

Looking up at the carving from under the chin, the block of wood should now look like this. Notice that the centerline is left untouched. This line represents the bandsawn profile and should remain intact until the very last stage of the carving.

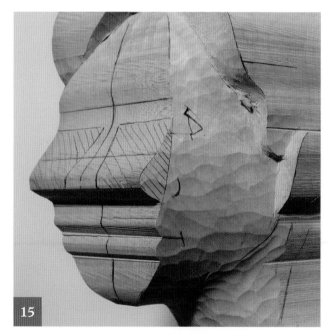

Draw in the positions of the eyes, nostrils and mouth on both sides of the carving. Measure the width of the nostril and the width of the bridge of the nose on both sides of the centerline. Then, on the side of the face, draw a line from the top lip to the top of the nose. Draw lines to show the approximate wedge shape of the nose.

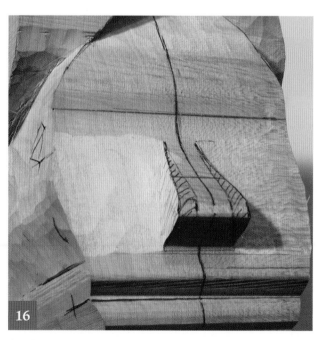

Cut the waste wood away into a square corner each side of the nose. Two triangular wedge-shaped pieces must be removed to give the nose a tapered shape.

Sculpting the Female Face & Figure in Wood   **43**

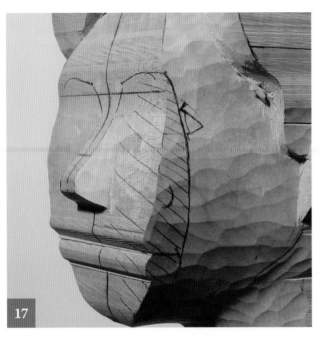

17

We now have to abandon our square cutting policy. Draw in the eyebrows by measuring upward from the mouth. Then draw a line on each side of the face from the end of the eyebrows, passing over the front surface of the eyelids, and down the cheek to the chin. Mark this area to be removed.

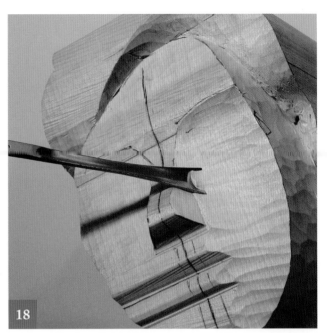

18

Working from the nose outward, scoop away the waste at the front of the face down to the level of the line that you drew down the cheek. These cuts will leave a curved corner between the nose and the cheek. Leave the central areas of the lips and chin untouched.

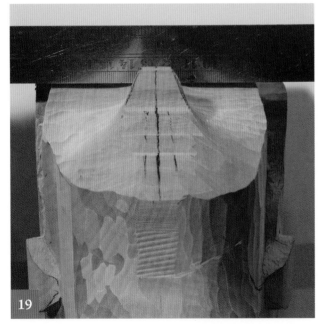

19

Use a straight edge to check that the areas around the eyes are flat and perfectly level. These two surfaces will become the front extremities of the eyes.

20

Mark the waste wood to be removed from the hard edges of the face.

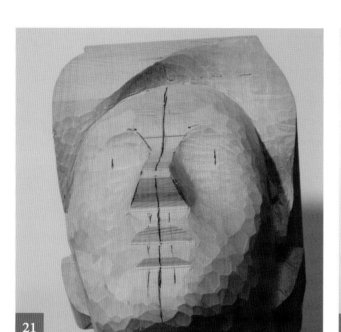

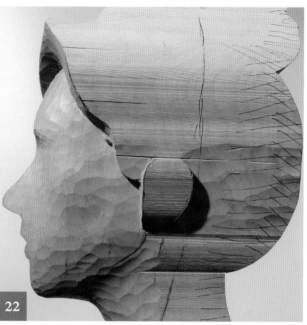

21 Round off the corners of the face from the hairline to the chin, shaping the face neatly and cleanly into a semi-circular form that becomes more pointed toward the chin. Ensure that both sides are perfectly symmetrical. Notice that the wood at the centers of the eyes has not been touched.

22 Mark the waste wood to be removed from the back of the head. Round the back of the head from the widest point just above the ears to the center of the back.

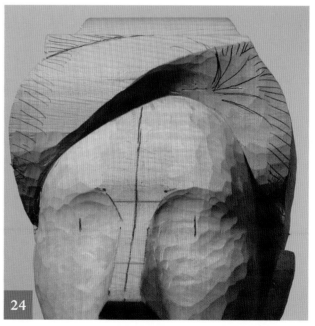

23 The back of the head and neck should look like this. The basic shape of the head is now established. Notice that the centerline remains.

24 For what looks like a simple enough hairstyle, this spiralling shape is quite difficult to grasp. The left side must be rounded down into a smooth curve. The right side sweeps back at the side and fans out onto the top surface. Let your gouge follow the lines of the hair.

Sculpting the Female Face & Figure in Wood **45**

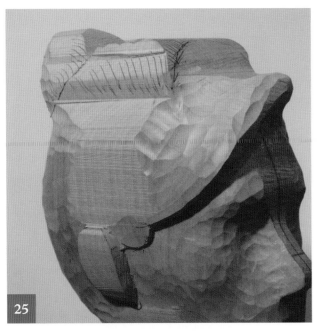

Mark the waste wood to be removed from the bun on the back of the head as shown.

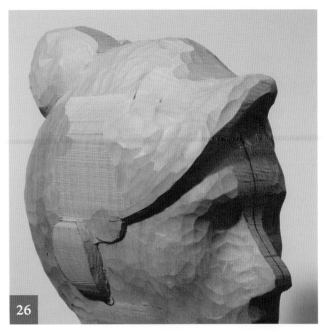

Round the bun on the back of the head into a ball. Remove the waste area in front of it to the line of the main shape of the head. The hair should now look like this.

ESTABLISH THE FEATURES

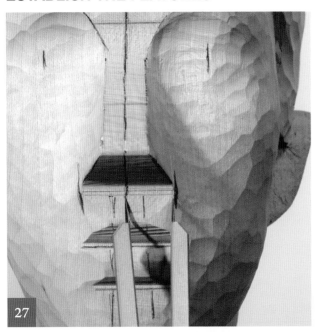

We now move to the second phase of the carving: establishing the details of the features. This requires very precise measurements and exact cuts. Maintaining the symmetry of the face is most important. First, measure the width of the nostrils from the centerline outward.

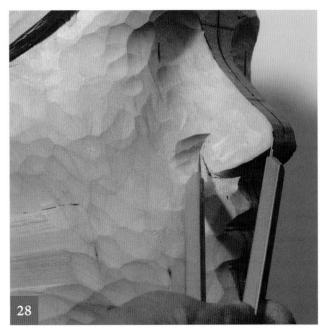

Now measure the length of the nose from the tip to the back edge of the nostrils. Cut away the cheek with a gouge until the required length of nose is achieved.

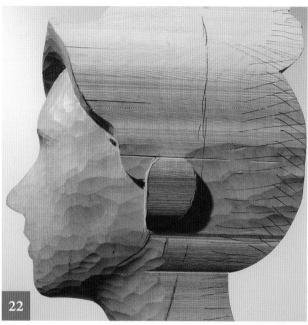

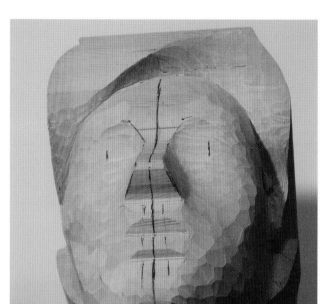
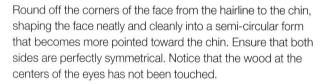

21

Round off the corners of the face from the hairline to the chin, shaping the face neatly and cleanly into a semi-circular form that becomes more pointed toward the chin. Ensure that both sides are perfectly symmetrical. Notice that the wood at the centers of the eyes has not been touched.

22

Mark the waste wood to be removed from the back of the head. Round the back of the head from the widest point just above the ears to the center of the back.

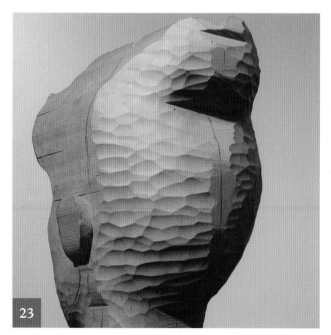

23

The back of the head and neck should look like this. The basic shape of the head is now established. Notice that the centerline remains.

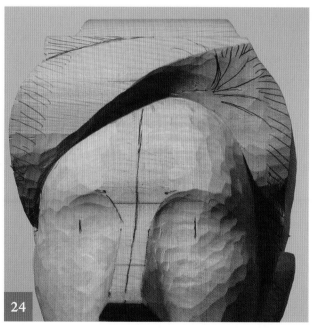

24

For what looks like a simple enough hairstyle, this spiralling shape is quite difficult to grasp. The left side must be rounded down into a smooth curve. The right side sweeps back at the side and fans out onto the top surface. Let your gouge follow the lines of the hair.

Sculpting the Female Face & Figure in Wood   **45**

25

Mark the waste wood to be removed from the bun on the back of the head as shown.

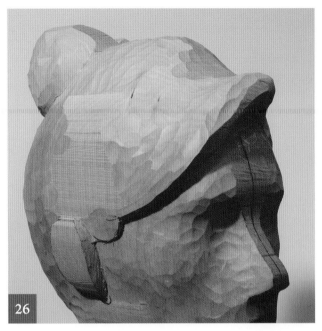

26

Round the bun on the back of the head into a ball. Remove the waste area in front of it to the line of the main shape of the head. The hair should now look like this.

ESTABLISH THE FEATURES

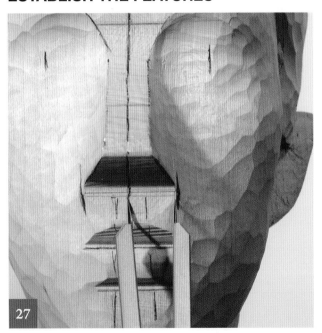

27

We now move to the second phase of the carving: establishing the details of the features. This requires very precise measurements and exact cuts. Maintaining the symmetry of the face is most important. First, measure the width of the nostrils from the centerline outward.

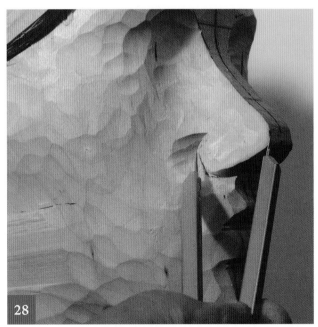

28

Now measure the length of the nose from the tip to the back edge of the nostrils. Cut away the cheek with a gouge until the required length of nose is achieved.

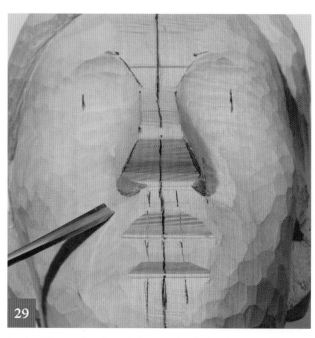

Look at the carving from below to check that the two sides are level. Blend the area around the nostrils into the cheeks with a gouge.

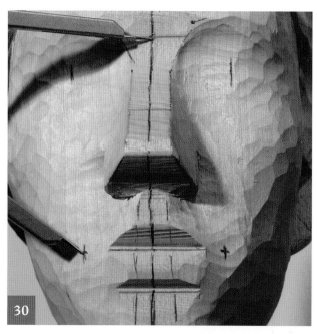

Now establish the line of the mouth. Measure from the center of the mouth to one corner; mark this length on both sides. Then measure from a point at the center of the forehead to the corner of the mouth. Where this point intersects the width measurement is the precise corner of the mouth.

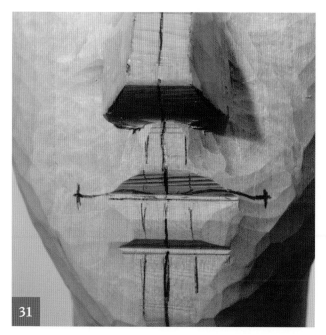

The method of measuring presented in Step 30 ensures that the mouth is at a right angle to the centerline. Now draw in the bow-shaped line of the mouth. Note that the indentations for the mouth and the chin are original bandsaw cuts.

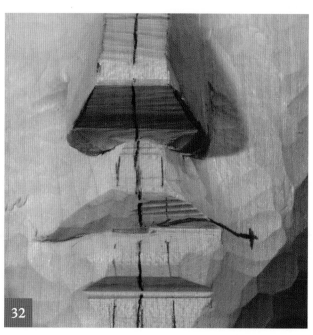

Using a number 3 gouge, cut in the upper lip. Repeat this cut on the opposite side.

Sculpting the Female Face & Figure in Wood   **47**

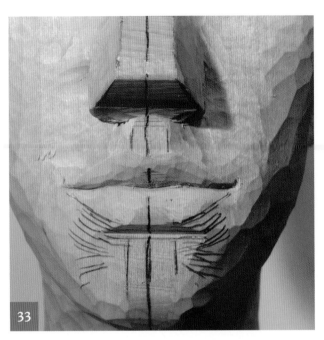

33

Shape the lower lip to meet the upper lip. Note that the centerline remains on both the upper and the lower lip. Then mark the waste wood to be removed below the lower lip at the sides of the chin.

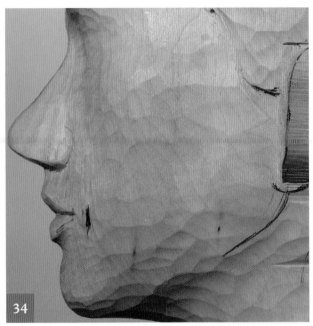

34

Look at the carving from the sides and compare it to the drawings. Here, the corner of the mouth does not come around the face as far as it should. It should extend approximately to the level of a line dropped from the front of the eyes.

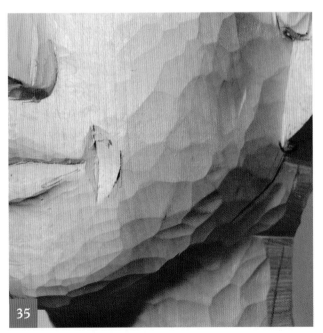

35

To rectify this, the mouth must be curved more tightly. Using a gouge, cut across from the true level of the corner into the cheek to the width of the mouth.

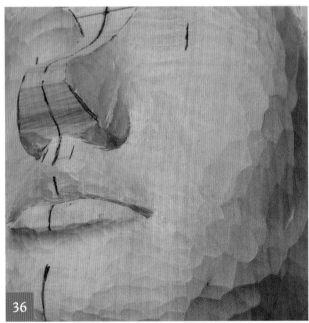

36

Now re-cut the curve of the mouth to this point and reshape the lips.

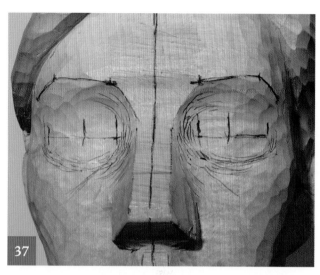

Draw in the eyebrows by taking careful measurements from the centerline (for width) and from the center of the lips (for height). Mark the width of the eyes by measuring from the centerline to the outside corners of the eyes, then from the outside corner to the inside corner. Now measure from the center of the lips to the inside corners of the eyes and draw a horizontal line across the eyes. This gives you the precise position of the horizontal axis of the eyes.

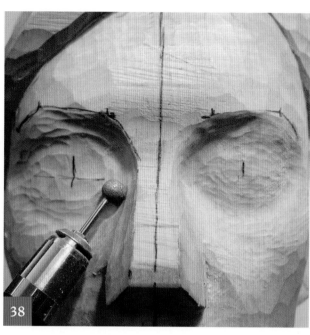

Remove some wood around the eyes to create two raised domes. I find the easiest way to do this is to use a ¼" ruby bur. Pay particular attention to the inside corner against the nose as this area is quite deep.

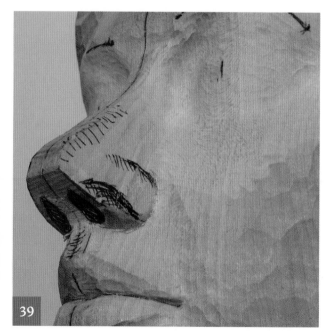

Moving to the nose, first mark the wood to be removed from the front and then mark in the nostrils. Looking at the photos of the model (pages 27–37) you will see that the nostrils slope upward and outward from the center.

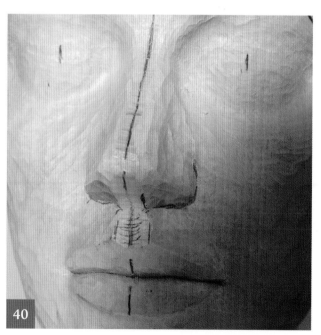

Round the front of the nose and cut the nostrils. The nose should now look like this.

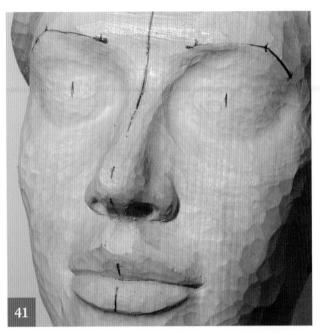

Drill out the nostril with a small round bur. The curve at the back of the nostril should not be a deep, hard cut but a soft, rounded groove. This is best achieved with a small diamond bur. Some slight hollowing above the nostril can be done with a shallow gouge.

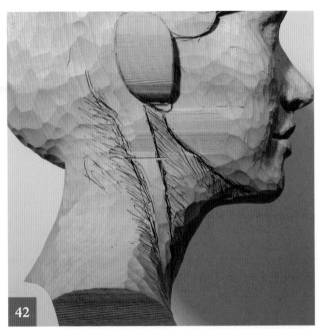

Mark in the jaw line and the sterno-mastoid muscle. This muscle is particularly pronounced on the model. (See the photo on page 29.)

DETAIL THE FEATURES

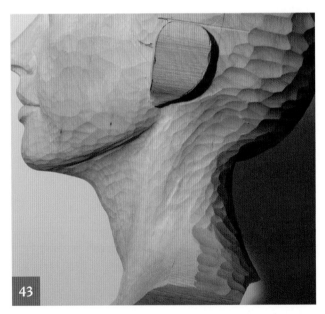

Shape the throat with a half round gouge. Notice that the area behind the ear has also been reduced where it narrows quite sharply. The main shapes of the face are now complete.

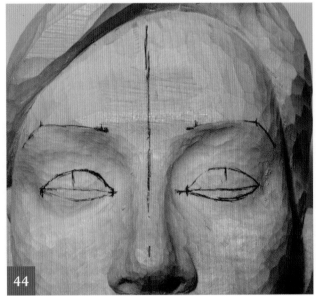

Draw in the eyes along the horizontal line. Using a very sharp gouge that fits the long curve of the upper lid, make a stop cut by pressing the blade in at a slightly upward angle under the lid. (You may need a different gouge for the tighter inner curve of the lid.)

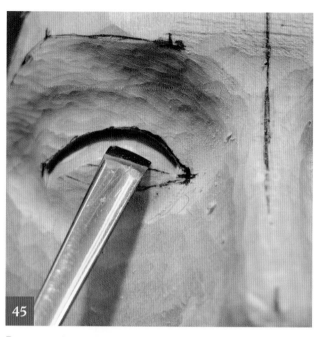

Pare away the waste on the upper half of the eyeball up to the stop cut using a flatter gouge.

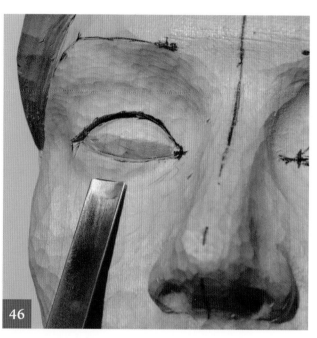

Repeat this operation on the lower lid, but make the stop cut square to the eyeball. This will leave you with a prism-shaped eyeball.

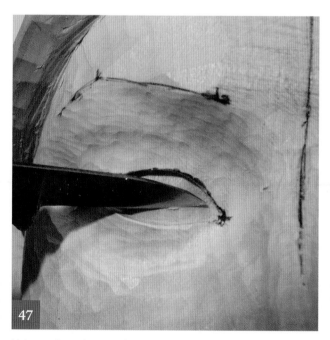

Using a sharp, long, pointed knife, pare the eyeball down to a curve, going deep into the two corners.

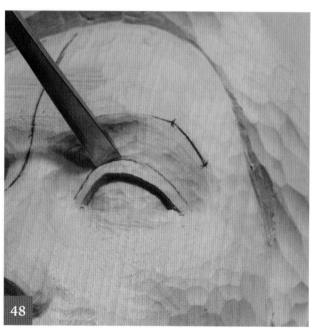

Cutting the crease of the upper lid is virtually a repeat of cutting the upper lid. First make a stop cut.

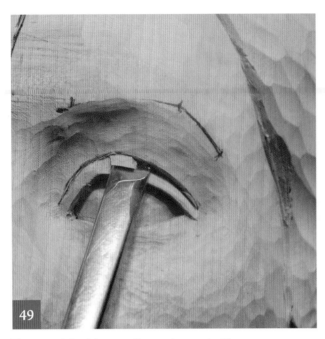

49

Then carefully chip away the waste wood with a shallow gouge.

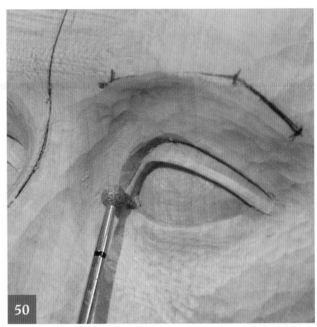

50

Invariably the hollowing of the inside corner of the eye socket is not deep enough and the lid will seem very thick. Reshape this with a ruby bur until the lids are a uniform thickness.

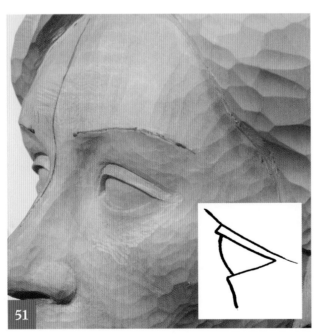

51

The eye is complete. Check that the eyelid forms a clean plane from the side view. The eyeball is tilted slightly forward with the upper lid well in front of the lower one. The edge of the eye socket is modeled to blend into the cheekbone and temple area. Some hollowing is needed below the cheekbone.

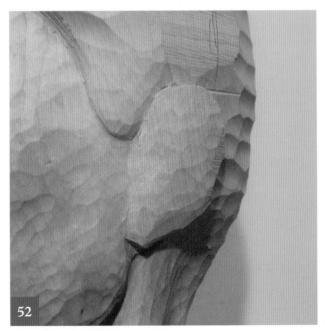

52

Shape the back of the cheek. It curves inward slightly in front of the ear. The back of the jawbone curves inward quite sharply below the ear and the neck is considerably thinner than the head. Shape the block for the ear so that it slopes inward from the widest point at the back down to the level of the cheek at the front.

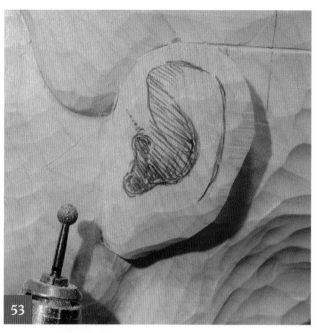

Draw the main details on the ear. It is easiest to carve the ear with a small, round ruby bur.

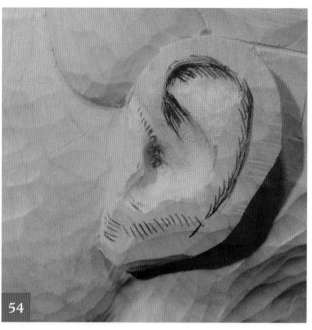

Rough out the largest cavities. The tighter corners will need a smaller bur.

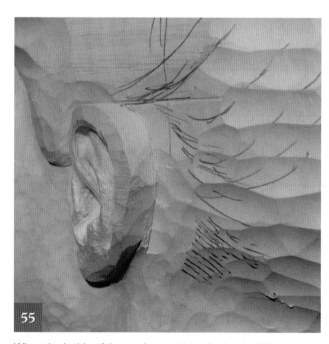

When the inside of the ear is complete, the back of the ear must be shaped. The skull behind the ear drops away very sharply, making the ear wider at the back than it appears at the front.

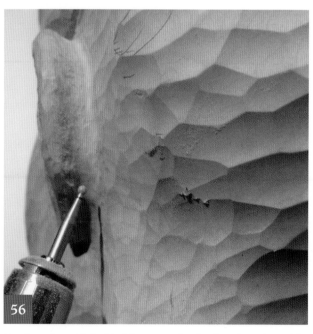

Use burs to cut in behind the ear, not going too deep to avoid making a hole.

DETAIL THE HAIR

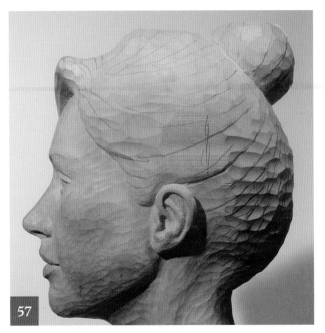

57

Now that the features of the head are complete, draw in the main lines of the hair.

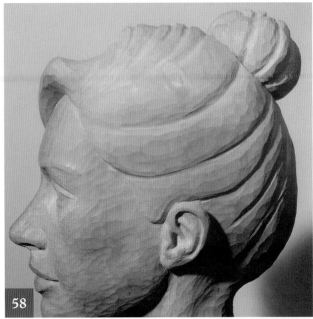

58

Cut the lines in deeply with a number 11 gouge—not a v-tool—and round over the edges.

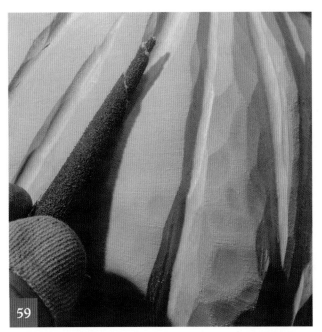

59

Begin the sanding process, starting with the hair. Using a good quality 80-grit sanding cloth rolled into a tight cone, remove all the tool cuts from the hair.

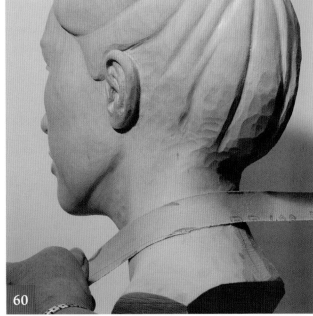

60

Large convex areas, such as the back of the neck, can be smoothed rapidly using a long strip of sanding cloth.

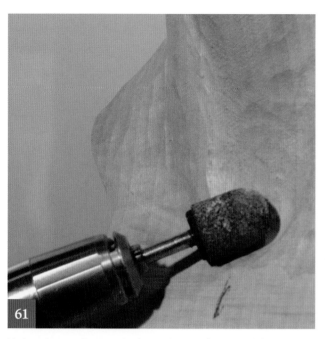

61

Various types of power tools can be used to speed the sanding process. This thumb sander is an excellent tool for cleaning out small hollows, such as the inside corner of the eye sockets.

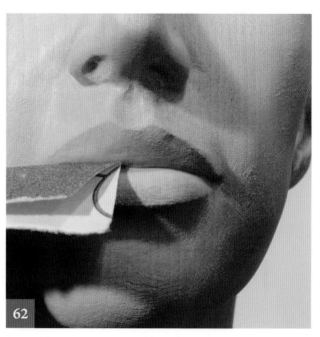

62

Sharp corners are best cleaned up using folded sandpaper. I find garnet paper is the best, as the grit does not flake off too much when the paper is folded.

63

The corner between the bun and the hair must be tidied up by creating a clean meeting point between these two areas. Cut the larger areas with a flat gouge, but use a small number 9 or number 11 gouge to cut the grooves in the hair.

64

The gouge must be ground back so that it will cut into a tight angle without the corners digging into the upper surface.

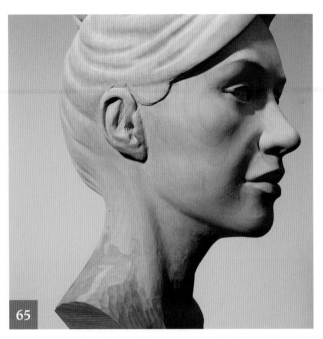

65

It is vitally important that tool cuts are completely ground away with the 80-grit sandpaper. If they are not, the finer grits of sandpaper will ride over the depressions and the tool marks will reappear when the final polish is applied.

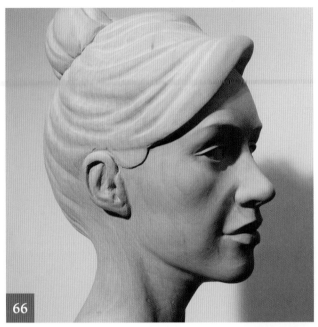

66

Here, the head is completely rough sanded except for the ear. Finish the ear with diamond burs.

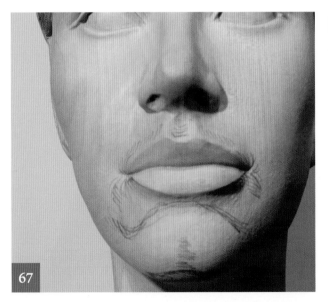

67

The finer shapes around the mouth are most important. The lips curl outward, so a small amount of wood must be removed above the top edge. The lower lip curls over sharply and disappears into a deep hollow at the corner of the mouth. On both side of the chin, a shallow depression curves downward and back up to the corner of the mouth. There is also a slight depression in the middle of the chin.

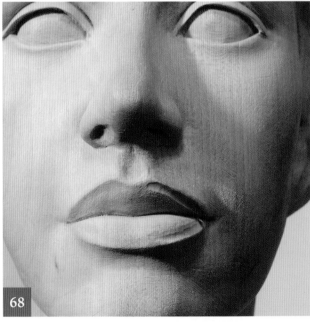

68

Cut a small shallow groove just inside the edge of the lips and carefully sand it to add an edge to the lips.

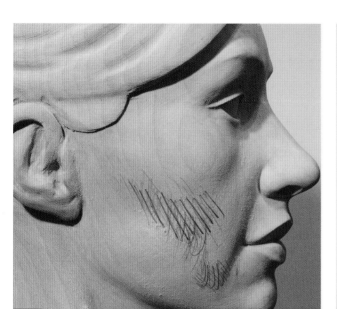

69

Looking at the carving from the side, you'll see that a touch more hollowing below the cheekbone and some slight shaping below the corner of the mouth are required.

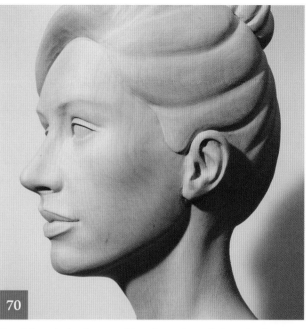

70

Sand the whole piece working down through the grits. I use 80, then 120, then 150 and finally 180.

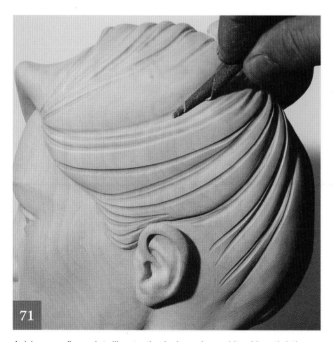

71

Add some finer detailing to the hair and sand it with a tightly rolled sanding cloth.

72

The head should now look like this.

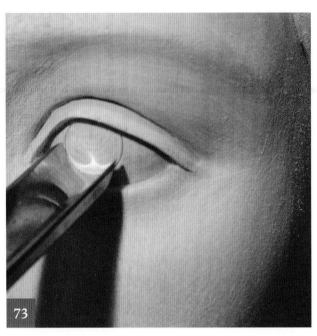

We must now cut in the irises. Make a circular cut using an appropriately sized half round gouge.

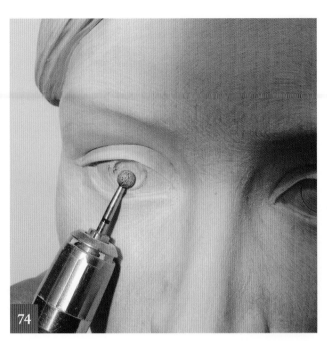

Using this circular cut as a guide, create a saucer-like depression with a round ruby bur.

The first stage of the iris is complete.

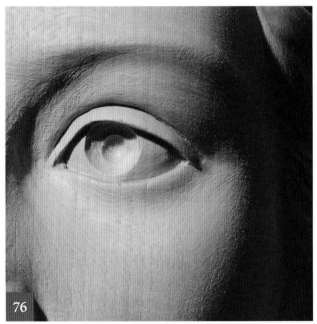

Now, using the bur, make a deeper hollow in the center of the iris for the pupil.

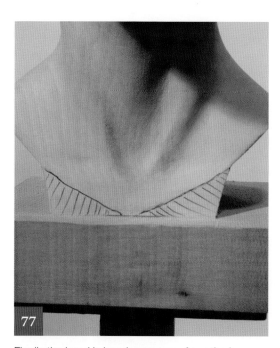

77

Finally the head is bandsawn away from the base. The front forms a point with a small flat area in the back for mounting.

78

Final sanding can now be carried out through 240, 280 and 320 grits. I prefer a durable, matte, clear and permanent finish. To achieve this, I brush on a coat of clear, matte polyurethane varnish, then wipe it off with paper towels. This leaves a very smooth surface free of brush strokes and runs. I repeat this three or four times. The finished carving is mounted on a block of walnut.

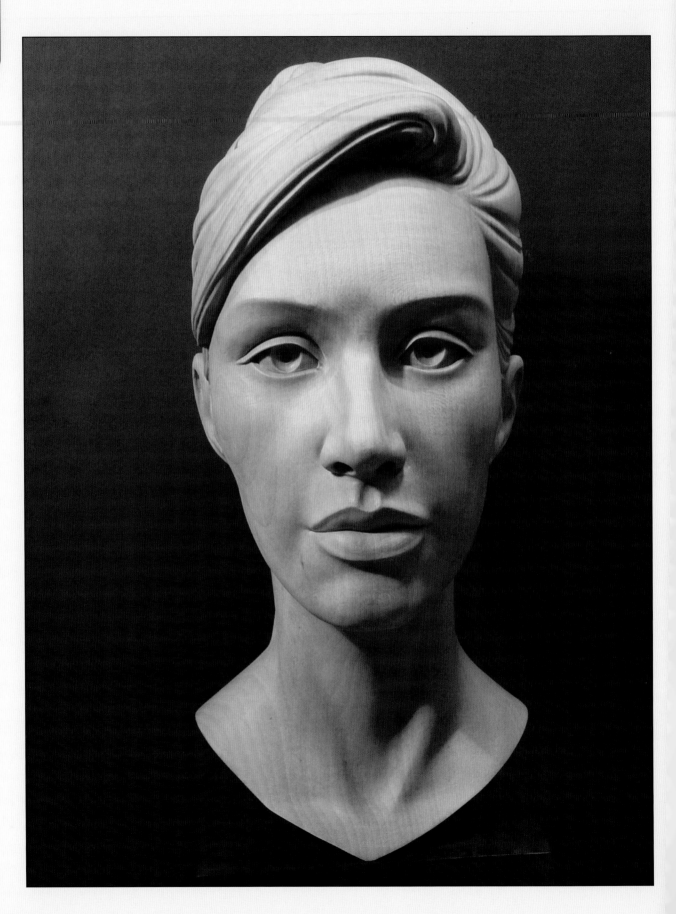

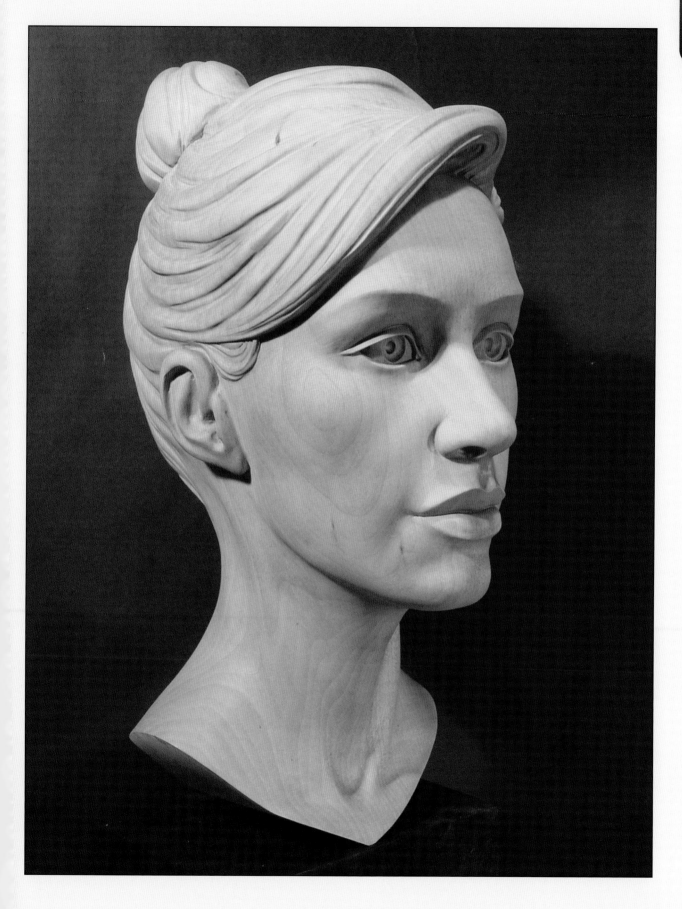

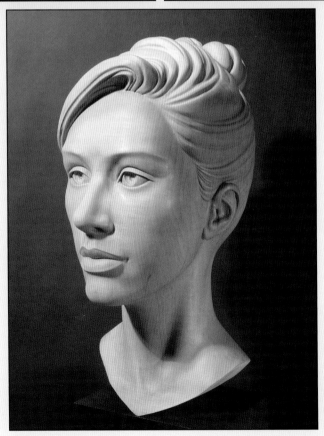

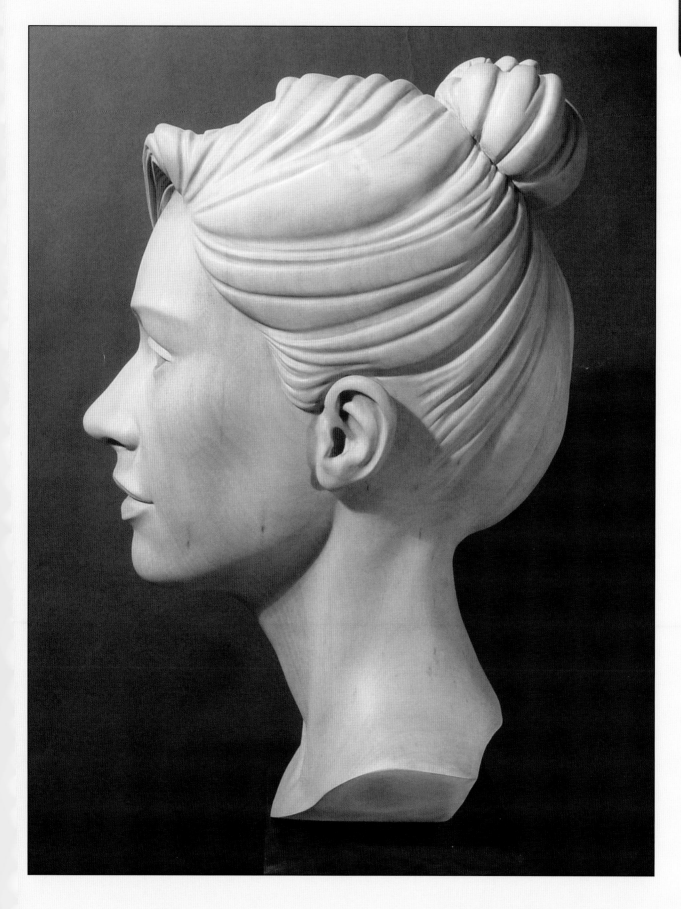

CHAPTER 3

Carving a Classic Afro-Caribbean Woman's Face

Nathaly is a very beautiful young woman from the Dominican Republic. Looking at the photographs, no particular feature is outstanding, and yet everyone who sees her is captivated by her face. Perhaps it is in some way the personality of the individual that adds the something extra that catches our attention.

Whether Nathaly's features are typical of the women in her country or of some area of Africa where her ancestors originated is uncertain, but the difference between her face and the European woman's face are quite clear. Those differences will be explored in this chapter.

CHOOSING WOOD

Wood for carving is always a problem. Obtaining timber in dimensions large enough for relatively small pieces is difficult and expensive; for larger sizes—over six inches square—it means using green (wet) timber, laminating or buying freshly sawn (green) wood, and carefully drying it for many years (one inch per year of thickness

is normal), and accepting that it may well split wide open. The portrait head is not particularly large, but to make it twice the height of the drawings on page 69 would require a piece of wood 7" x 8" x 14" high, even without the ponytail.

I particularly wanted to make this piece from dark, figured, European walnut. To obtain timber this size, I buy core logs from veneer factories. These are cylinders of wood that are left over when the veneer making process is finished and measure about a yard long and vary in diameter from six to eight inches. Although they usually have flaws, such as dead knots, bark inclusions or pieces of metal, they are inexpensive, dry and usually beautifully grained.

Walnut is a superb wood to carve, although it can be hard, and it is most satisfying when the final polish is applied, revealing the beautiful marbling, ripples and flames that seem almost translucent. It is well worth the effort.

FACE PATTERN: AFRO-CARIBBEAN WOMAN

CARVING A CLASSIC AFRO-CARIBBEAN WOMAN'S FACE

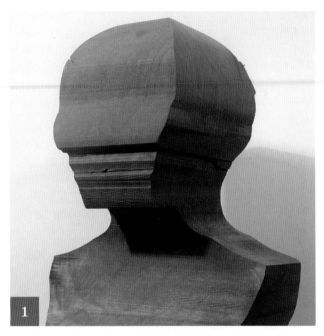

The blank for this project is bandsawn in the same way as the first project except that the ponytail is made separately. This process allows a much smaller piece of wood to be used and enables the back of the head and neck and the inside of the ponytail to be carved more easily.

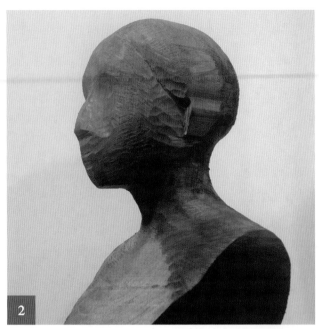

Following the same general procedures as the first project and using the pattern and the photographs as a guide, rough out the general shape. Much of the rounding can be carried out with a Surform rasp.

The main features are carved in. The strongly domed shape of the forehead is apparent. The eyes are heavy lidded with an extra fold of skin on the top lid. They also slant upward and outward. The fold below the eyes is also quite strong. The nose is broader and less pointed than a European, and the cheekbones are fuller and more rounded. The lips are more generous and curvaceous.

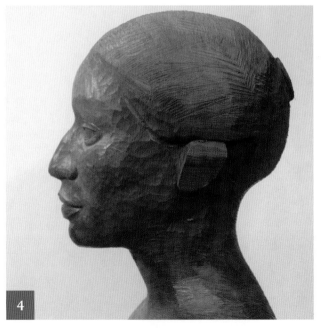

From the side the round forehead is clear, as is the slightly aquiline nose. The lower part of the face is slightly more forward in relation to the forehead than that of the European model.

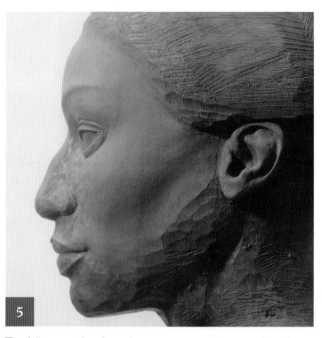

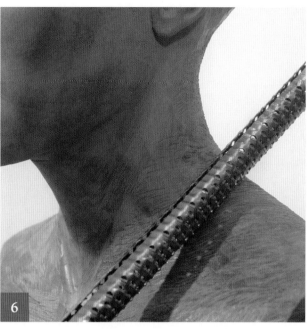

5

The fuller, rounder shape becomes more apparent when the piece is sanded. Notice also the shorter, rounder ear.

6

Walnut can be very hard. It is easier to achieve large, rounded surfaces with a rasp.

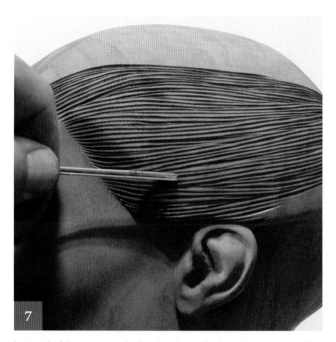

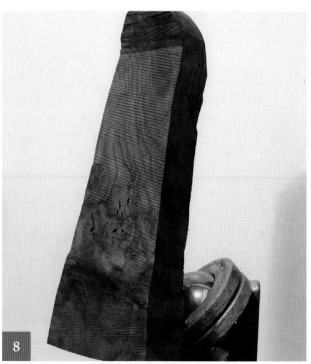

7

Instead of the cornrow hairstyle shown in the photographs of the model, I decided to "v-tool" the hair instead. This is rather tedious and requires a steady hand, but the tool marks lend a pleasant textural contrast to the sanded face.

8

Screw the bandsawn block for the ponytail to the clamp in an area that will later be cut away during the shaping of the hair.

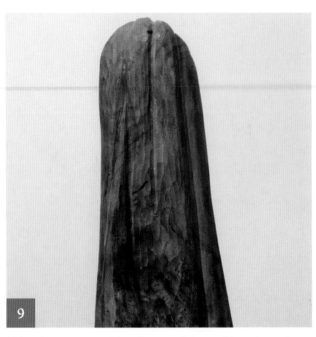

9

Using the pattern and the photographs as guides, shape the back of the ponytail.

10

The sanded ponytail is ready for texturing.

11

When all of the hair is textured, glue the ponytail in place with a dowel.

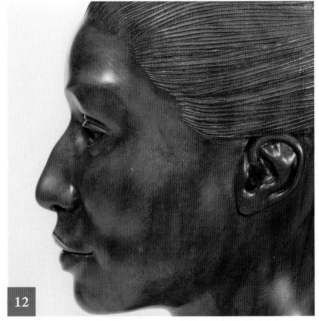

12

Polish the carving with three coats of matte polyurethane varnish. The finished piece is beautiful, although it has ended up more shiny than I would like. I will cover the joint on the ponytail with strips of heat-treated and patinated copper that hang like ribbons over the shoulders. These give a pleasant contrast to the walnut.

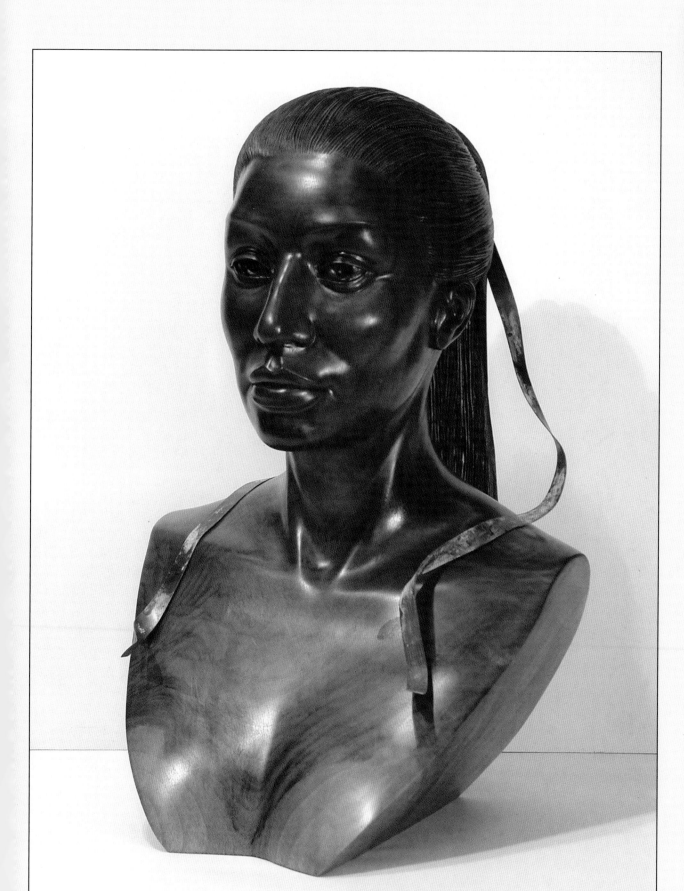

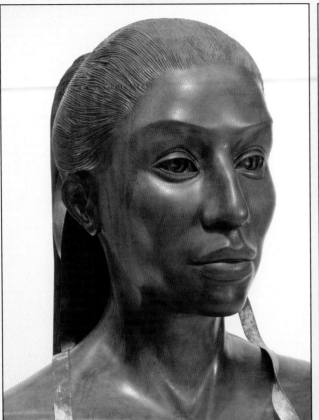

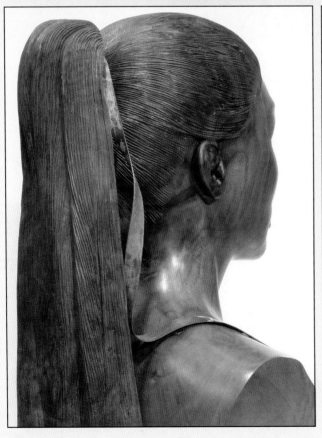

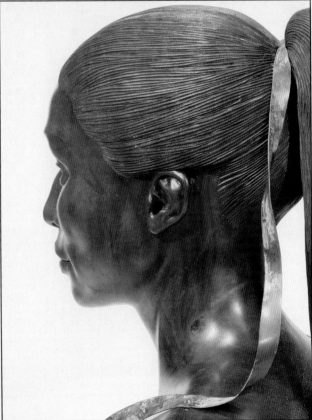

CHAPTER 4

Carving the Samburu Girl

The Samburu are a tribe living just above the equator in northern Kenya, Africa. Like their better-known relatives, the Maasai, the Samburu have resisted European culture and maintained their ancient way of life. Their young women are exceptionally beautiful.

This carving is an example of the problems involved in carving a bust when the head is turned to one side. To make this carving with the head turned and the shoulders square required a block of walnut 7½" x 11" x 15", which is quite large. To bandsaw it with the face pointing forward and the shoulders turned would have required a block 9" thick, which was unavailable. This meant that the blank could not be bandsawn accurately and that the shaping had to be done by eye, which was far more difficult than the process of shaping a bandsawn blank, as shown in the previous two projects.

In this chapter I provide the final patterns and photographs of the finished piece. By using these patterns, which were made after the carving was finished, you can create a carving that follows the same basic process as the previous two projects.

FACE PATTERN: SAMBURU GIRL

© IAN NORBURY

© IAN NORBURY

CHAPTER 5

Carving a Girl's Face

The difference between the face of this four-year-old child and an adult woman is obvious to anyone, and yet when a carver tries to analyze the differences, they become rather elusive. The face is softer and fatter; the whole shape is more square; the eyes are slightly larger; and yet, one could find an adult with the same features, but it would still look like an adult. We, as carvers, can reproduce the shape of the head in wood, but capturing the childlike quality in the subject may be more difficult.

The first problem begins with taking the photographs. The pictures of the adult in Chapter Three, Donna, who is a professional model, were taken in a studio by a skilled photographer. Most carvers will have to make do with amateur snapshots of untrained models. Children are far more difficult to persuade to pose in a certain way, and it is even more difficult to pose them in the same position for subsequent photographs.

Thus, when I sat down to carve Julia, I was faced with a collection of photographs, of which only several were good enough in and of themselves. Notice that these photos are not in alignment: The front view is looking down at the subject. This meant that I had to use a larger block of wood than would normally be required. However, this is typical of the type of problems that occur all the time in carving real people, and we have to overcome them.

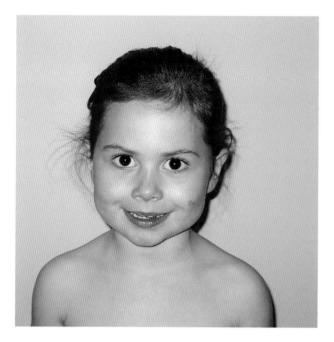

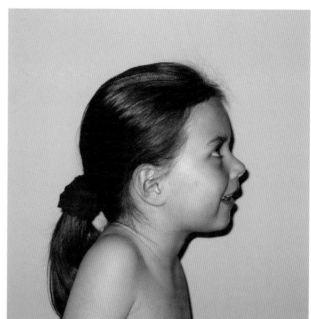

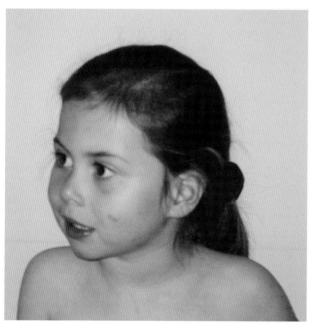

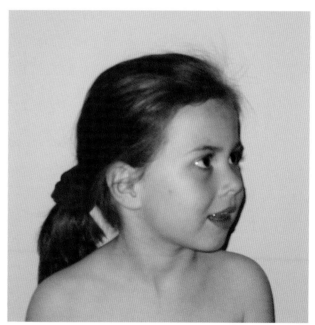

FACE PATTERN: GIRL

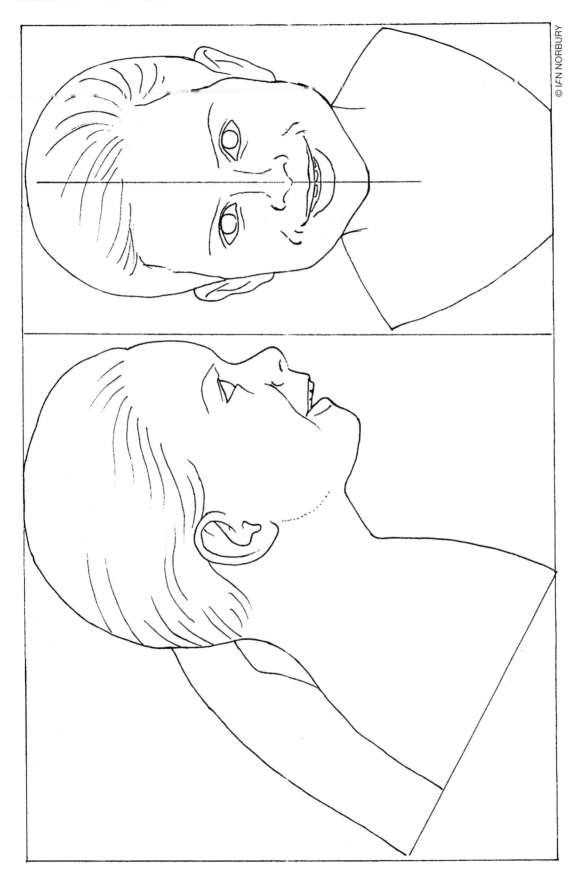

© IAN NORBURY

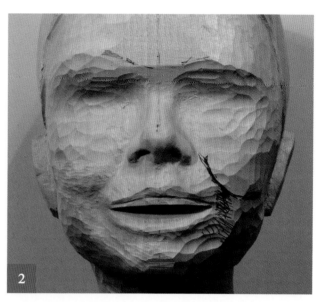

Bandsaw the head in the same manner as the previous projects. The first difference from the adult head occurs when removing the waste from the eyes down the front of the cheeks. On the adult this is almost a flat surface, but on the child, it bulges forward where the cheeks are much fatter.

Notice that the neck is very thin and that features such as the jawbone are very soft and indeterminate. The nose is flatter and less ridge-like than that of the adult, with the sides forming shallow slopes. It is only fractionally wider than the adult's, but the nostrils are very prominent. The shape of the cheeks and corners of the mouth are quite different, partly because of the fuller cheeks. The fuller cheeks are due partly to the smile.

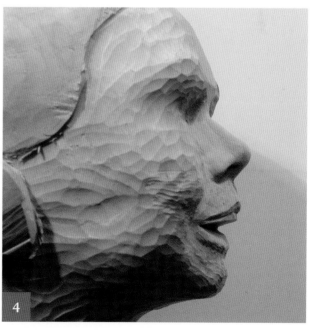

The eyes are set quite deeply between the brows and cheeks. The eye-bag below the eye is also proportionally larger than that of the adult. There is a depression running under the eye-bag and around the cheek, which is caused by the smile. This can be seen clearly on the profile of the three-quarter picture.

From the side, the deep set of the eye and the initial shaping of the cheeks can be seen.

Sculpting the Female Face & Figure in Wood   **83**

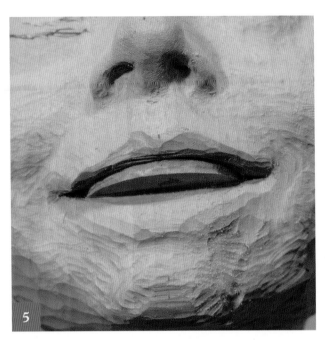

The first stage in shaping the teeth is to cut them well back from the lips and deep into the corners of the mouth. Remember that the teeth are much narrower than the mouth.

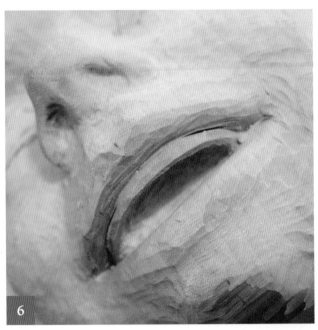

The second stage of cutting the teeth is to hollow out the inside of the mouth with a bur, undercutting the back of the teeth.

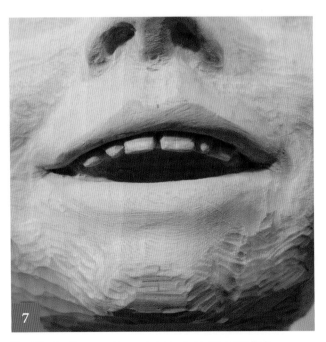

Next the teeth are cut in and shaped, and the top lip is deeply undercut.

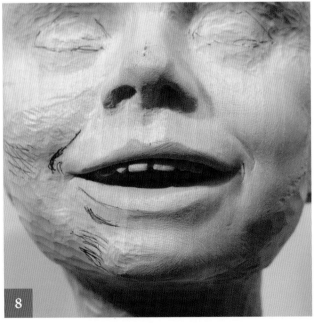

The shaping around the mouth is quite complex as a result of the interplay of muscles in the smile. The slight shallow creases are cut in with a small v-tool.

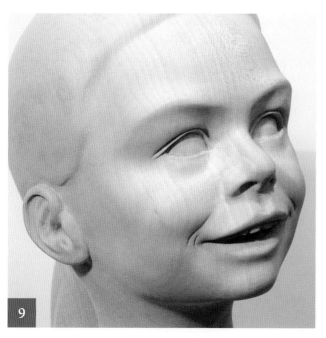

9

The head has been rough sanded and is ready for the finishing touches.

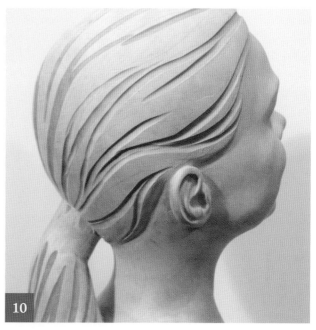

10

The first stage in carving the hair uses a #11 gouge. Notice that the cuts are unevenly spaced—not a regular distance apart, which results in a mechanical appearance.

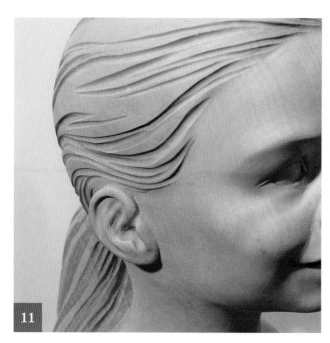

11

The second stage in carving the hair uses a much smaller #11 gouge to introduce more detail. Notice that the cuts must be long and flowing. Precise positioning is less important than achieving the flowing lines.

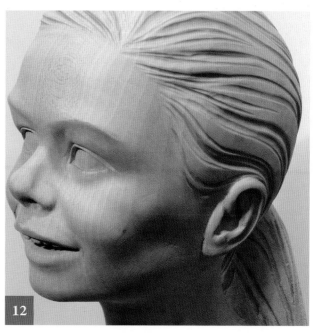

12

In the final stage of creating the hair, the cuts have been softened using 240-grit sanding cloth. This treatment of the hair gives the carving a less formal appearance than the carving in the first project.

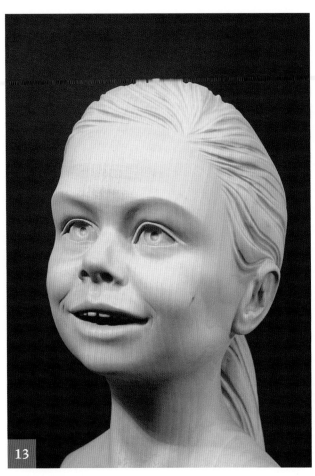

13

The carving is sanded through 120-, 150-, 180-, 240- and 320-grit sanding cloth.

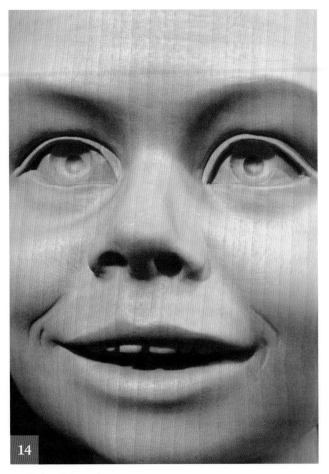

14

The irises are made with burs using the same process as described in Chapter Three.

CHAPTER 6

Carving a Torso in Limewood

The actual removal of wood on a torso is very simple. Much of it can be carried out with a couple of gouges or even a rasp. It is not knowing which bits to cut off that creates the problems.

I have not included a tool list for this project because your choice of tools will change depending on the size of your carving. Any reasonable selection of gouges will be sufficient to complete the torso shown here.

By carefully carrying out this project, you will gain a greater understanding of the form of the torso and the underlying structures and, perhaps most importantly, acquire a systematic method of working from a concept through the various stages to a finished piece. This method can be applied to many more projects.

Limewood has many great advantages. In Europe, it is a very common tree, particularly in cities where it seems to thrive on concrete and smog. It grows to a great girth, has no discernable sapwood, mills easily, and dries quickly with little splitting. Because of its cell structure, it carves more easily than any other wood I know and will take the very finest, delicate detail. It sands to a fine finish and stains and polishes well. Basswood, if not the very same tree, is certainly a very close American cousin and is, for all intents and purposes of this book, identical.

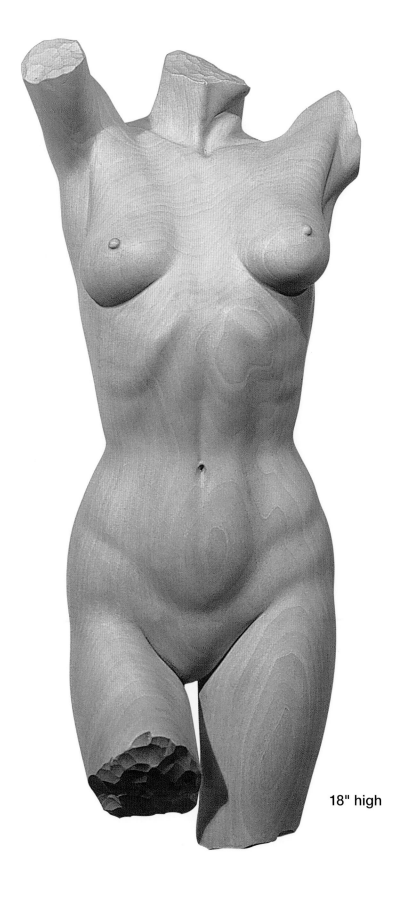

18" high

Sculpting the Female Face & Figure in Wood   **91**

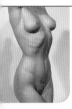

Reference Photos

These photographs of a professional model (pages 92–95) were used to create the patterns for the limewood torso shown in this chapter. Use these photos as reference as you work to complete the step-by-step carving project.

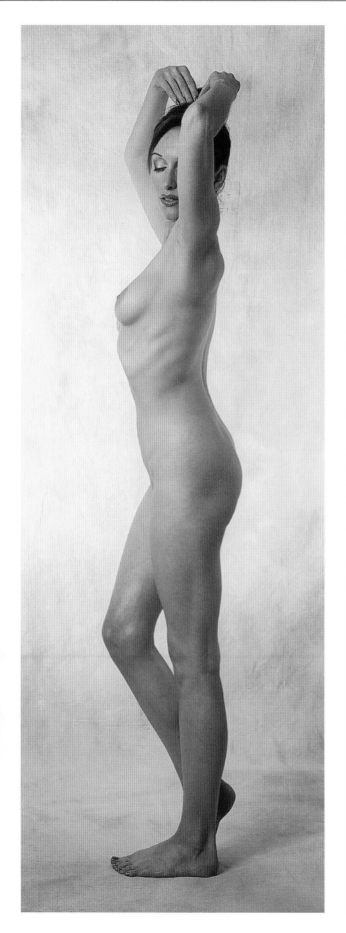

Sculpting the Female Face & Figure in Wood   **93**

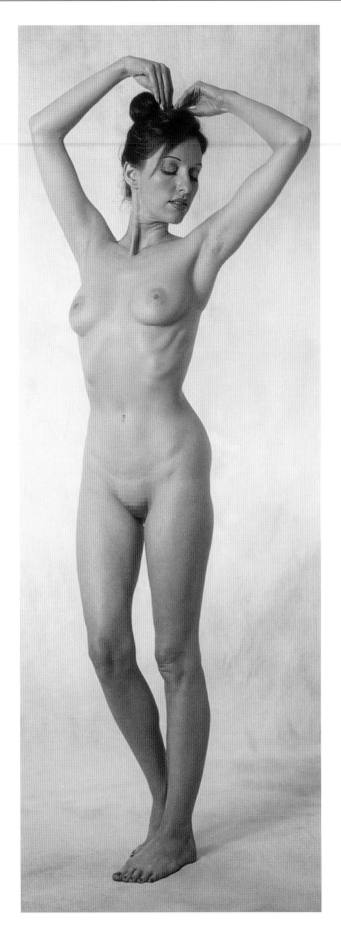

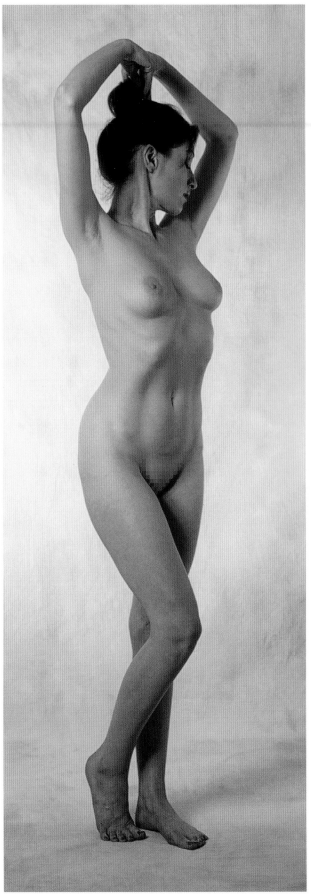

LIMEWOOD TORSO

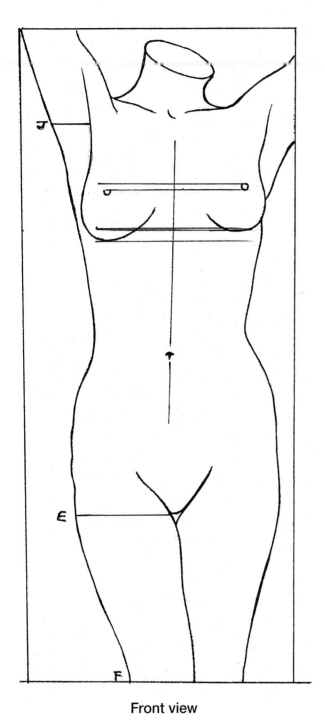

Front view

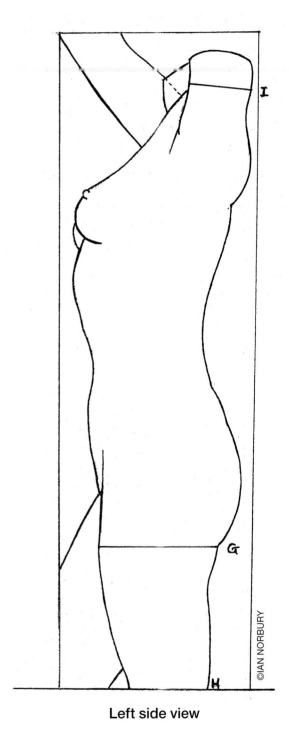

©IAN NORBURY

Left side view

Use the front and side views shown here to bandsaw the blank. Cut very carefully, precisely on the line. Remember that tracing the plans onto a block of wood and bandsawing them allows for considerable accumulative errors. Only by taking great care can you reduce these errors to a minimum.

LIMEWOOD TORSO

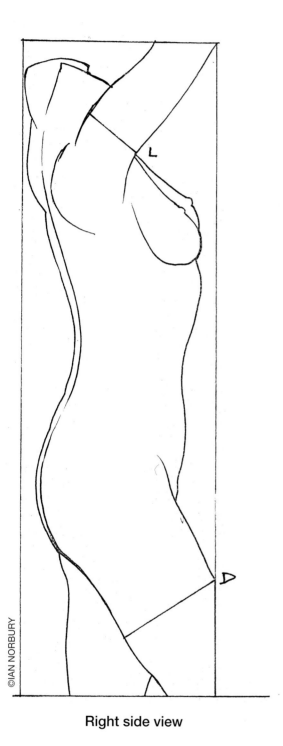

©IAN NORBURY

Right side view

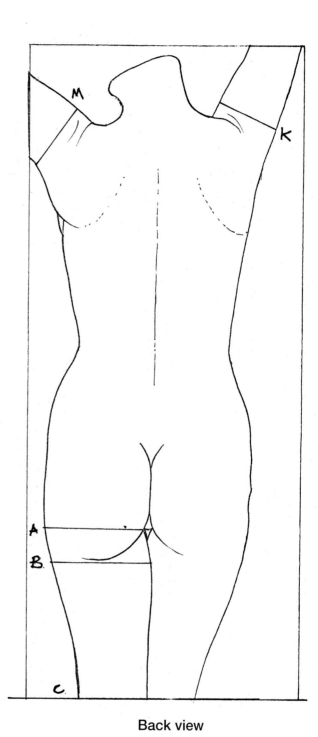

Back view

The back and opposite side views are provided to show carving details.

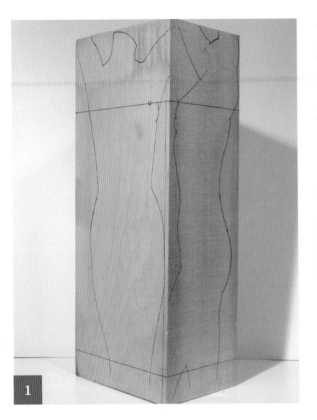

Enlarge the drawings to fit the size of wood you choose. My block is 19" x 5½" x 7½". The block must be planed perfectly square or the bandsawing will be inaccurate. Trace the front and the right-side drawings onto two adjacent sides of the block. Use the right nipple as a datum line to align the drawings. Only the outline is needed. Leave a piece at the base so the carving can be held in a vise or clamp.

Note: The words "left" and "right," when used throughout the demonstration that follows, always refer to left and right as seen on the figure from the front. Therefore, what appears to be the left side when looking at a photo of the back of the carving is still referred to as the right side.

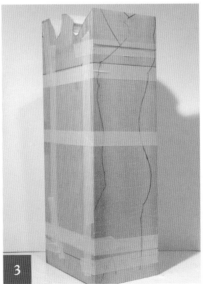

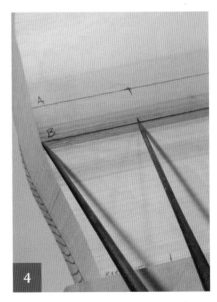

Bandsaw the front view. Notice that the cut is as close to the line as possible, thereby ensuring that the dimensions of the sawn blank are identical to the drawings. Make sure the bandsaw blade is perfectly square to the table. Always follow the manufacturer's safety instructions.

Use masking tape to securely fasten the two main pieces of waste in place. You are now ready to make the second cut. More tape will need to be added during the bandsawing process as areas are cut away.

The main areas of waste must now be marked on the wood. Mount the blank on a vise or clamp. Using a pair of dividers, measure the dimensions of the limbs. First measure the positions lines A – H on the patterns (pages 96 and 97). Mark the lines on your carving and then measure the width of the limb at those points. Measure and draw precisely, not approximately.

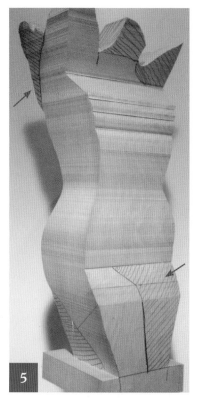

Mark the waste wood to be removed on the right leg. This area is in front of the leg that is pushed back. Also mark the waste wood to be removed behind the left shoulder.

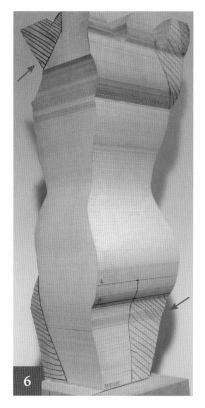

Mark the waste wood to be removed from the back of the left leg. This area is behind the leg that is pushed forward. Also mark the waste wood to be removed in front of the right shoulder.

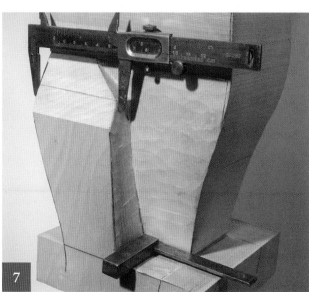

Start to remove the waste using a half round gouge, then flatten the surfaces with a flatter gouge. The waste in the corner of the legs at the back and at the front must be cut into a neat square corner. This ensures that the dimensions remain the same throughout the widths of the limbs.

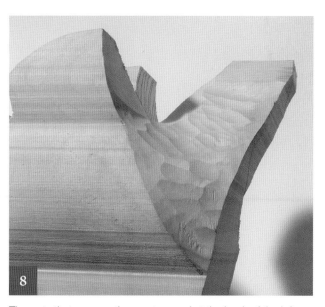

The cuts that remove the waste wood at the back of the left shoulder must curve from the shoulder up to the line of the neck, then taper away to the line of the shoulder blade. (See Step 5.) The cuts at the front of the right shoulder (See Step 6.) and at the front right of the neck also have to curve up the neck (See Figure 26.). Check the sizes of the upper arms using lines I–L. M and K should be the same and I and L should be the same.

Sculpting the Female Face & Figure in Wood **99**

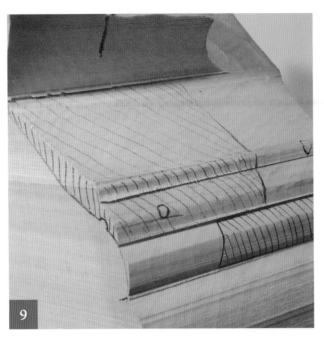

9

The right breast is slightly higher than the left, because the left arm is angled forward, the right arm is pulling upward. Remove a small amount of waste below the right breast to raise it; remove a small amount above the left breast, to lower it. Mark the waste wood to be removed above the left breast. Remember to leave wood for the nipple, as shown.

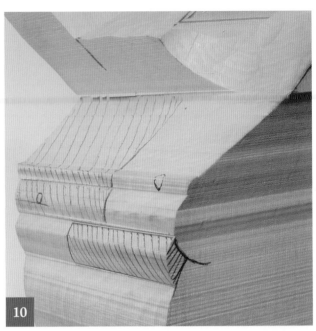

10

Mark the waste wood to be removed below the right breast.

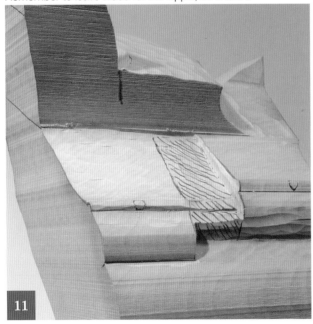

11

Next, mark the waste wood to be removed between the breasts.

12

Scoop out the area between the breasts down to the level of the breastbone, which runs in a straight line up the center of the chest.

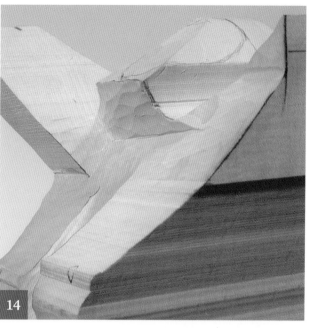

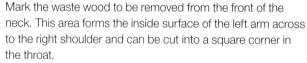

13

Mark the waste wood to be removed from the front of the neck. This area forms the inside surface of the left arm across to the right shoulder and can be cut into a square corner in the throat.

14

This area has now been removed. The area around the neck is the most complicated part of this carving and is hard to visualize. Careful measurement and precise cutting are vital. Mark the dimensions of the neck and draw the circular shape on the top.

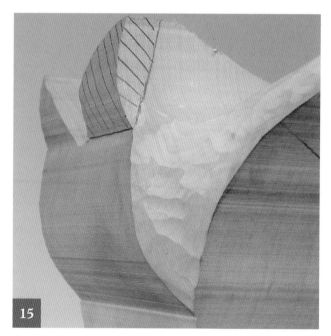

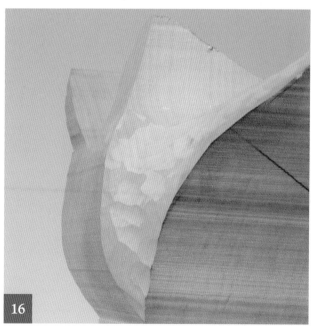

15

Now mark the waste wood to be removed from the back of the neck. This curved piece is the extension of bandsawing the shoulder.

16

This waste wood has been removed, and the neck should now have its true dimensions.

Sculpting the Female Face & Figure in Wood   **101**

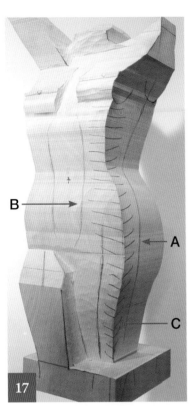

You can now proceed to round off the figure. Starting on the right side, draw a line from the highest points, running down the muscles around the shoulder blade, down the ribcage to the hip and thigh (A). On the front of the body, draw a line down the leading edge of the ribcage and along the side of the stomach muscles (B). Draw another line from the front of the hipbone down the middle of the thigh (C). You will also need to draw the side view of the breast.

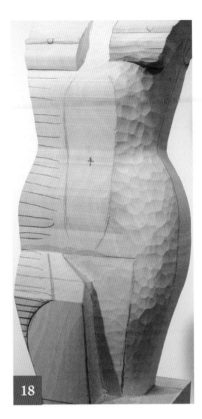

This corner from the bottom of the breast to the baseline of the figure can now be rounded off. Leave the centerlines untouched because they represent the profile the figure. You are basically trying to create a circular shape from a square one, so the waste wood you are removing should leave a quarter-circle. The completed cuts are seen here. Now repeat this step on the left side.

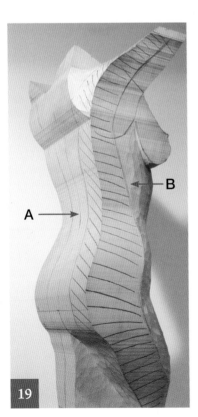

Draw a line down the center of the back of the left arm, running down the high point of the shoulder blade and down the column of muscle at the side of the spine, across the buttock and down the thigh (A). Draw another line down the outside of the left arm, along the rib cage, across the hip and down the thigh (B). Mark the wood between the lines for removal.

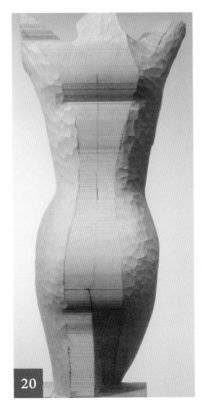

Round off this corner and repeat the procedure on the other side. The back of the carving should now look like this. Notice that the lines marking the high points are still intact.

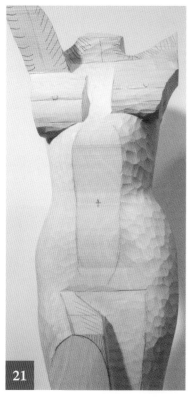

You now have to round off some minor areas at the front: the top inside of the left thigh, the two lower corners of the left arm, the top corner of the right arm and the front of the neck. Mark the waste wood in these areas for removal, as shown.

21

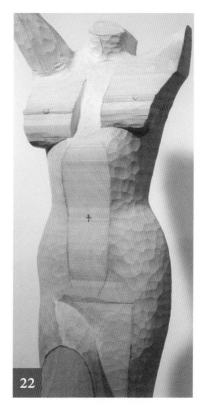

This stage is complete. Notice that the areas between the neck and the shoulders are scooped into curves rather than square corners.

22

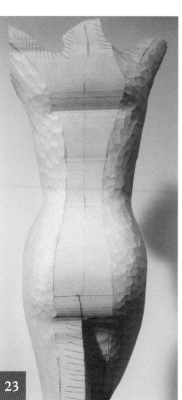

Returning to the back, mark the waste wood to be rounded off on the inside corners of both arms. This shaping runs into the shoulder and up the back corner of the neck. Also mark the inside corner of the right leg to be rounded.

23

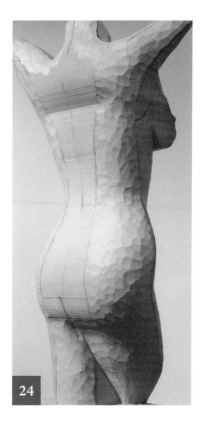

Remove the wood from these areas.

24

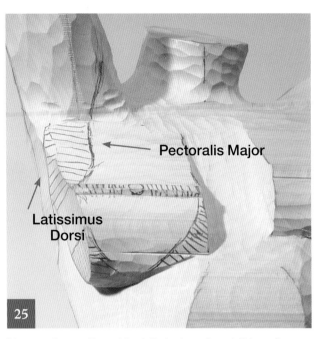

Pectoralis Major

Latissimus Dorsi

25

Measure the position of the left nipple and mark this on the carving. Then mark the lower inside and outside curves. Measure Line J (page 96) and mark in the line of the muscle from the upper arm to the breast. On the side, measure and mark the back line of the breast, running up to the armpit.

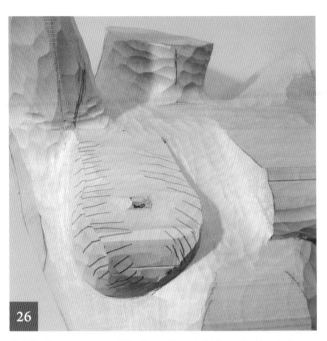

26

Cut the lower curves of the breast straight in to the level of the ribcage. The area at the side can be cut away, but leave a round gouge cut in the corner. The waste wood on both sides of the nipple is also removed. Finally, round over the two edges of the breast.

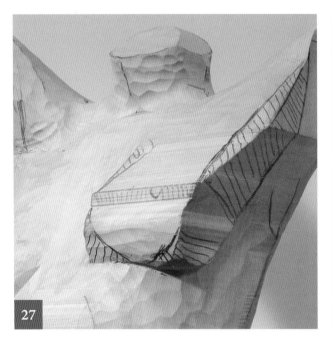

27

Mark the waste wood as shown and repeat this process on the right breast.

28

Notice that the breasts are mounted on the curve of the ribcage and point outward at an angle, not straight forward.

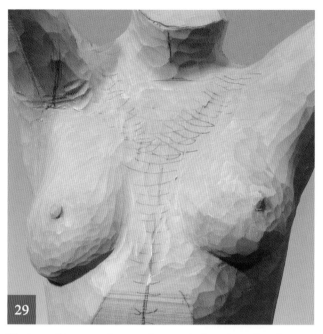

The breastbone, or sternum, forms a hollow down the chest, particularly near its lower end. This levels out toward the neck. The shoulder muscles, being raised, therefore, form the hollows between themselves and the neck. Together this forms a "Y" shape. Mark the wood to be removed.

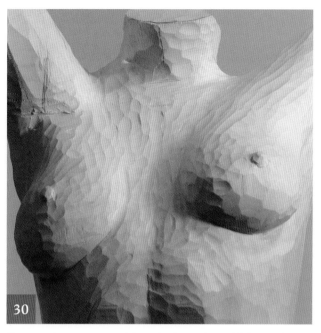

Remove the waste wood from the breastbone. This area is now complete.

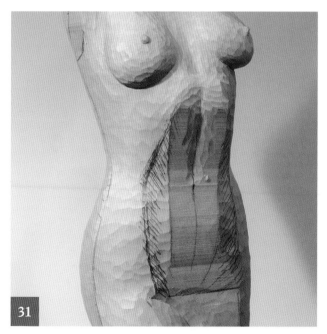

The stomach requires careful study. In the photograph on page 94, you can clearly see the ribcage curving outward and backward. In the center are the stretched stomach muscles. Below the ribs at the sides are two large muscles running down to the sides of the pelvis. Between these and the stomach muscles is a pronounced hollow. (See also Figure 8, page 24.)

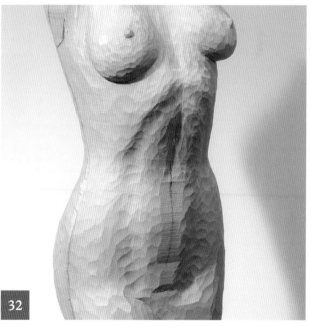

Following the markings, carve two large furrows running down the arch of the ribcage and down both sides of the stomach. Round off the stomach as it curves upward from these furrows. Leave the centerline and the navel as high points. Compare your progress with the photograph on page 94.

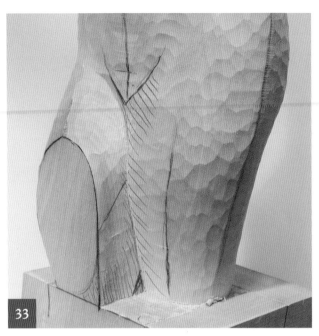

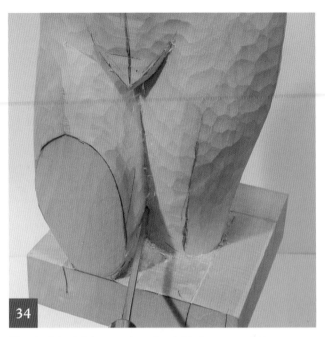

Moving to the bottom of the stomach and thighs, you can see in the photograph on page 94 that the thighs do not actually touch. The inside of the right thigh and the rear edge of the left thigh must be rounded to separate them. Mark the wood to be removed in these areas.

Clearly, if the left leg overlaps the right, the space between them must be at a slight angle.

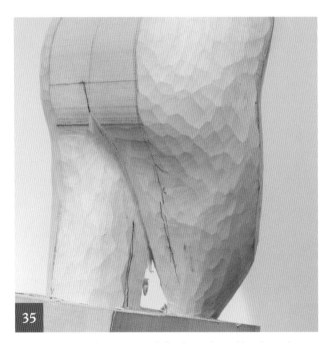

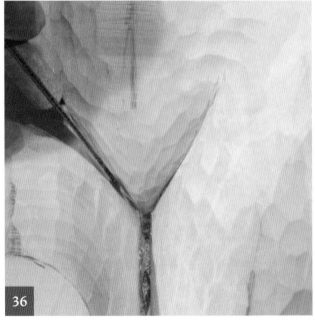

The thighs must be very carefully shaped, working from the back and the front to create the opening. If the cuts from the back and the front do not line up, a serious fault can be created.

As cuts for the opening reach the top of the thighs, remove wood from the pubic bone. It curves backward between the legs and is rounded over on both sides. The deep fold between the fat pad on the pubic bone and the bulge at the top of the thigh is cut in with a knife.

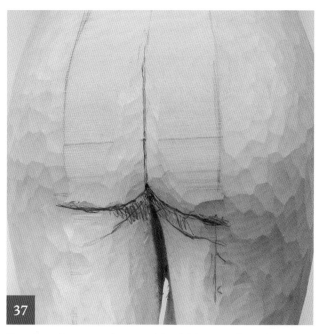

37

The triangular gap at the top of the thighs must be at the same height in the back and in the front. Measure this distance from the baseline and mark it on the centerline. Notice that the left buttock is slightly lower than the right because of the left leg's being thrust forward.

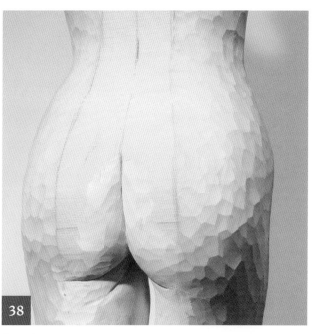

38

Completing the shaping of this area between the legs is very difficult. When the space is finally cut through, you may find it easier to shape and clean up with a strip of 80-grit sanding cloth.

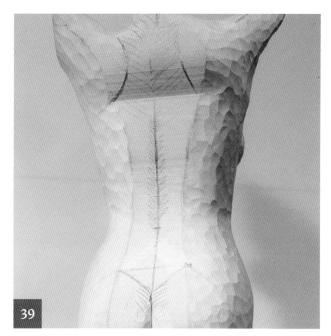

39

Mark the wood to be removed from the spine. At the top of the buttocks this is a deep cleft which quickly flattens out on the sacrum. This is best seen in the photograph on page 95. Just above the sacrum it becomes deep again between the two columns of muscles. Just below the shoulder blade it again starts to flatten out in a shallow depression between the high points of the shoulder blades.

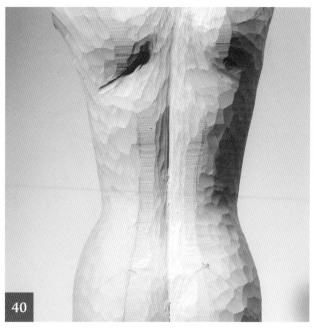

40

Remove the wood from the marked areas.

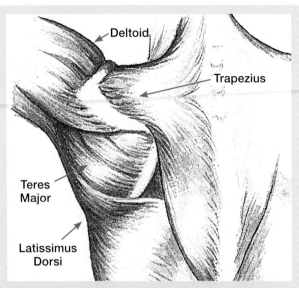

Diagram A: Note that the muscles of the upper back are extremely complex and react strongly to slight movements and stresses on them. They also vary dramatically according to the muscular development of the individual. This subject is only thinly muscled, and just below the neck the vertebrae can be seen protruding.

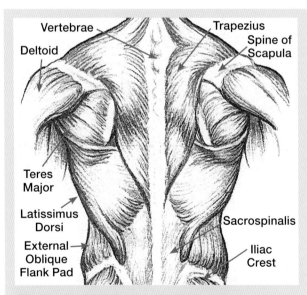

Diagram B: Where the shoulder blade meets the arm, you can see the large bulge of the deltoid muscle and the deep creases where the arm, shoulder blade and collarbone intersect. Notice the hard, straight edge of the trapezius muscle, which attaches to the top edge of the spine of the scapula and runs across the shoulder and up the neck.

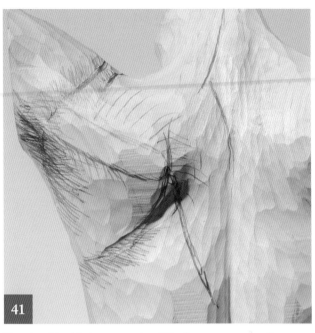

41

The shoulder blades present a difficult area, a mass of bones and muscles in constant movement. Study the photographs on pages 14, 15 and 17 carefully. The light line running diagonally across the shoulder blade (page 92, 93, and 95) is the spine of the scapula. The lower end juts out (page 92). The inner edge of the blade curves around from the inner end of the spine toward the outside of the body (page 95) and curves forward (page 95). Mark the waste wood for removal, as shown.

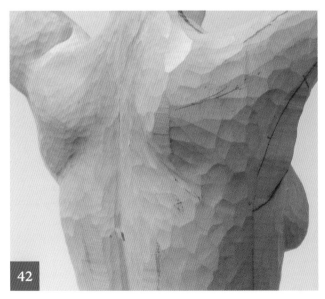

42

Having carved this area, carefully studying the photos along the way, now compare it with the photo on page 95. It is quite good, if a little lumpy.

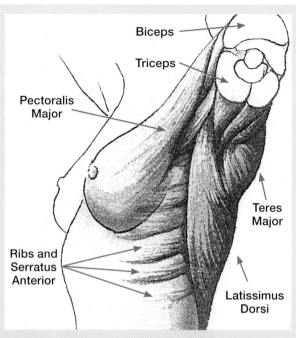

Diagram C: Moving to the front of the shoulder, you find an equally complex arrangement where the pectoral muscle rises up from the chest to engage with the deltoid muscle at the top of the arm. The muscles wrap around the front of the shoulder blade and fold in between the biceps and the triceps. In the triangle between the breast and the shoulder blade, the ribcage, thinly covered, slopes in toward the neck.

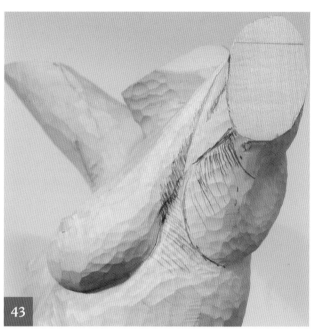

Mark the waste wood to be removed along the side of the breast, along the underside of the arm and on the front of the arm, as shown.

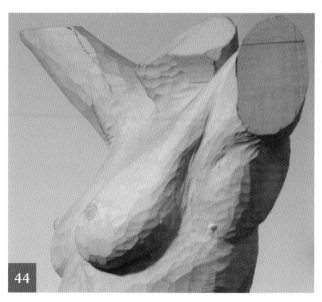

The wood has been removed from this area. Note the curved groove formed on the underside of the arm and the slight indentation on the front of the arm.

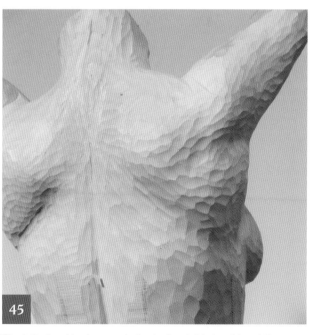

The left shoulder is very similar to the right shoulder at the back, but it is slightly further around the body because the arm is angled forward. The high point of the spine of the scapula is less prominent. The deltoid muscle is less swollen and the hollow between the deltoid and the shoulder blade is less pronounced because the arm is not angled upward as much.

Sculpting the Female Face & Figure in Wood   **109**

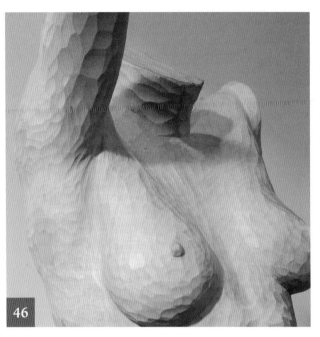

46

A view from the front shows the angle of the arm and its effect on the shoulder blade as it moves around toward the front of the body.

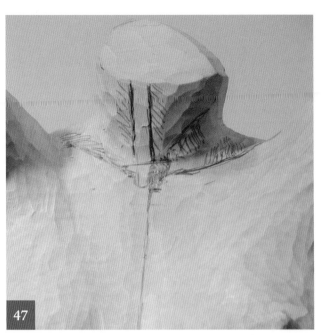

47

Mark the wood to be removed at the neck and collarbones.

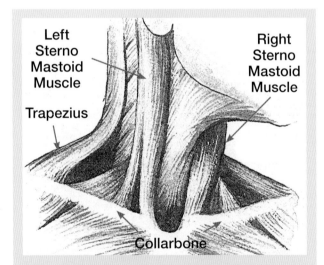

Left Sterno Mastoid Muscle

Right Sterno Mastoid Muscle

Trapezius

Collarbone

Diagram D: On this model, who has very little body fat and muscle, the left sterno mastoid muscle, running from the back of the ear to the inside end of the left collarbone, is exceptionally prominent. Because of the twist of the head, it runs perfectly in line with the central line of the body. The right sterno mastoid muscle is relaxed and twists from the end of the right collarbone, around the neck and out of sight. Between the two muscles, the windpipe can be seen cutting across at 45 degrees. The collarbones, clearly seen at the front, curve backwards and upwards, disappearing in the muscles of the shoulders.

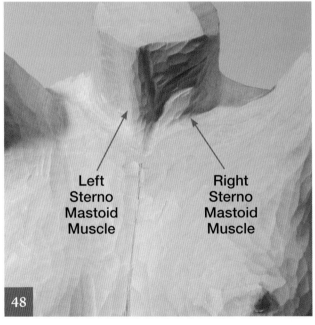

Left Sterno Mastoid Muscle

Right Sterno Mastoid Muscle

48

This area is now complete. Notice the translation of the left and right sterno mastoid muscles in the wood of the neck.

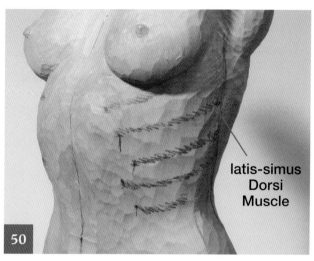

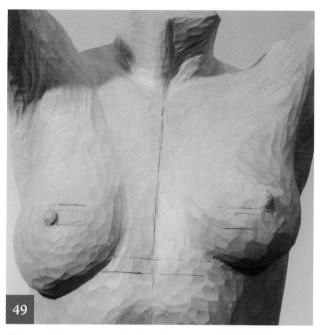

49

After carefully remeasuring the drawings and carvings, it became apparent that the left breast is considerably too low. The lower line on this photo shows the true level. The nipple is only fractionally too low and should be okay.

50

latis-simus Dorsi Muscle

The left breast has been raised. On the model the ribs are highly visible, even on the back in some views. If you carve everything as you can see it, the finished torso will look ugly. With this in mind, carve the ribs only as far back as the latissimus dorsi muscle, which runs from the armpit, down around the side to the pelvis at the back. Notice that the fourth rib, marked below the breast, is more prominent than the others.

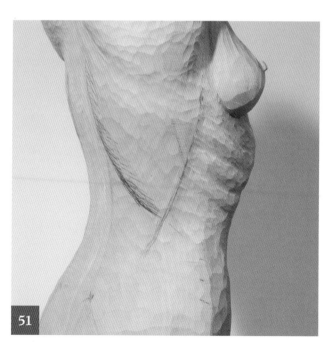

51

Carve in the ribs, and then move to the back. Looking at a photograph of the back (page 95), the shape of the ribcage can be seen as it passes under the column of muscle running up either side of the spine. Mark this area for wood removal.

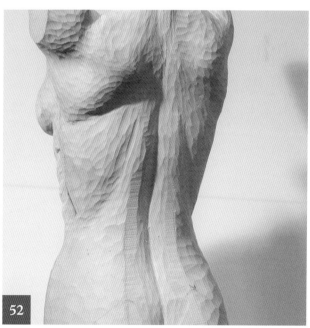

52

The wood has been removed, and the muscles on the spine can now be clearly seen. The line of the ribs runs down and around the side, sharpening the waistline.

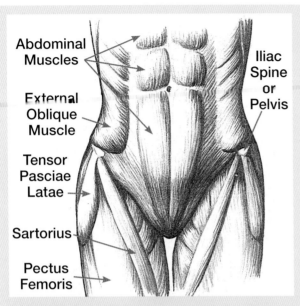

Abdominal Muscles

Iliac Spine or Pelvis

External Oblique Muscle

Tensor Pasciae Latae

Sartorius

Pectus Femoris

Diagram E: Some complicated and quite subtle shapes create the stomach and the hips. On both sides of the centerline are the abdominal muscles. Outside of these are the external oblique muscles that run up and over the ribs. The pelvis is tilted because the bent left leg raises the right corner of the pelvis slightly. The abdominal muscles run down to the pubic bone.

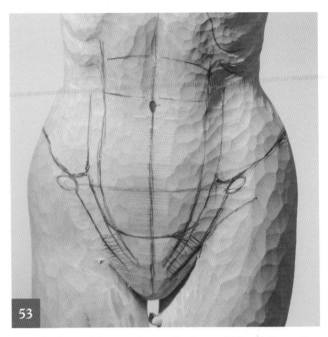

53

Mark the lines of the muscles on the figure. At the bottom of the external oblique, the front corners of the pelvis appear as two small oval lumps. The details can be seen fairly well in the photographs of the model on pages 92, 93 and 94.

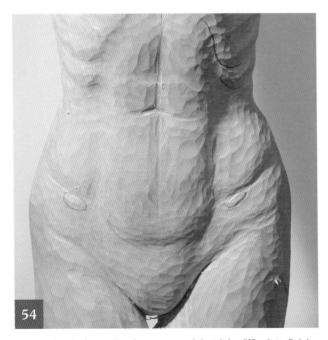

54

The abdominal area has been carved, but it is difficult to finish it completely in isolation from the hips and the thighs.

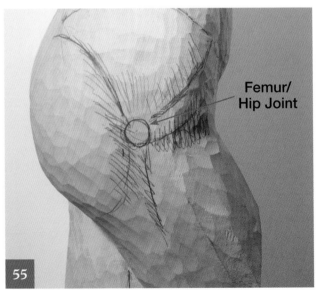

55

Femur/ Hip Joint

Mark the muscles on the left hip area. On the left side of the model there is very little definition of the muscle because it is not under tension. This lack of tension creates, more or less, a smooth, curved expanse of flesh. The crease where the leg folds is quite marked, however. The circle is the actual joint at the top of the femur that one can feel and see.

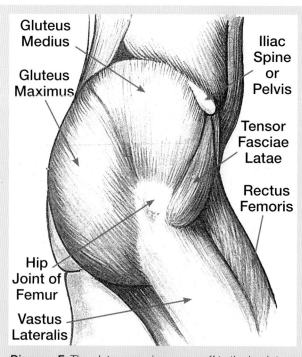

Gluteus
Medius

Gluteus
Maximus

Iliac
Spine
or
Pelvis

Tensor
Fasciae
Latae

Rectus
Femoris

Hip
Joint of
Femur

Vastus
Lateralis

Diagram F: The gluteus maximus runs off to the back to form the buttock and also upward to attach to the pelvis. At the front another muscle connects from the hip to the front of the pelvis.

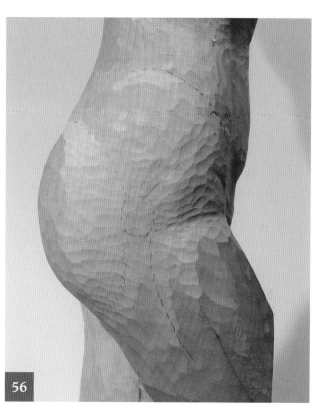

56

Here these areas have been carved.

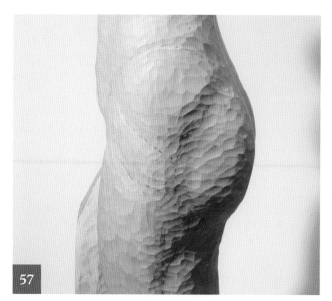

57

The structures on the right side are more clearly defined. The buttock is tightened to support the body, and this causes a deep hollow at the side. This can be seen clearly in the photograph on page 93. On this side there is also a large groove running down the thigh where the big muscles are in tension. Mark and carve these areas now.

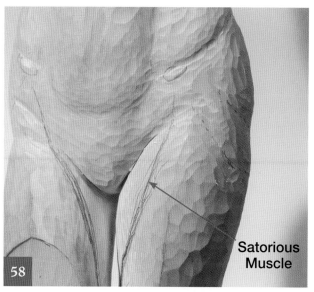

58

Satorious
Muscle

The final piece of shaping is the sartorius muscle, which runs from the front of the pelvis and twists around the front of the thigh to the inside back of the knee. Mark these muscles, as shown.

Sculpting the Female Face & Figure in Wood　**113**

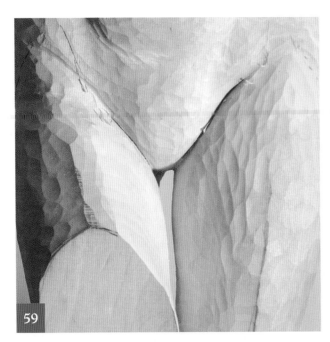

59

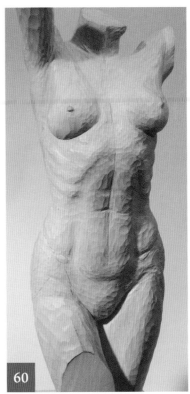

Your carving should now look something like this. If you are a staunch adherent to the tooled finish, you have the difficult task ahead of achieving a surface in keeping with the skin of a young woman. For my own part, I now sand the entire carving with 80-grit sandpaper to achieve a smooth surface.

60

The sartonius muscle is a very subtle form. It can be seen in the photograph on page 94 and quite clearly in the photograph on page 92. Although not a strong shape, it does give the characteristic shape to the thigh. Note that the centerlines down the legs still remain.

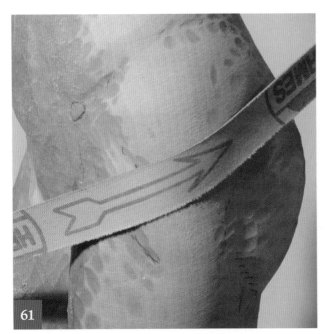

61

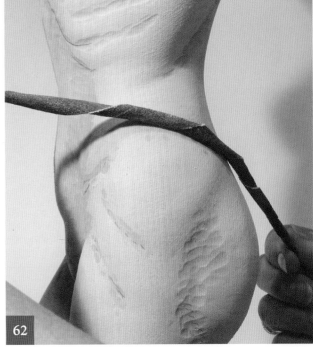

62

Using a strip of quality 80-grit sanding cloth, sand the figure to a uniformly smooth surface. The remains of tool cuts, such as can be seen here, must be totally removed. If they are not eradicated with the coarse grit, they will probably still be there when the polish is put on.

Some of the depressions can be sanded by twisting the strip into a tube or by using narrower strips.

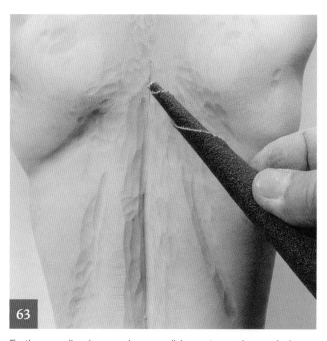

63

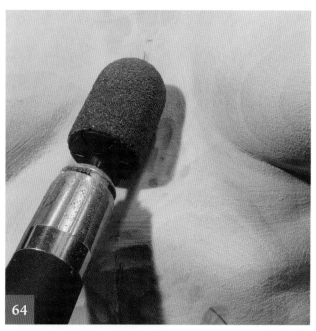

64

Further sanding in more inaccessible spots can be carried out using a square of cloth rolled into a cone. The sanding up to this point has taken exactly one hour. Using good quality materials and the right methods, sanding does not take as long as many people think.

In some hollows and grooves, power tools, such as the thumb sander shown here, can be used to remove the tool cuts. Take great care if you use this method, and do not expect these tools to produce a finished surface.

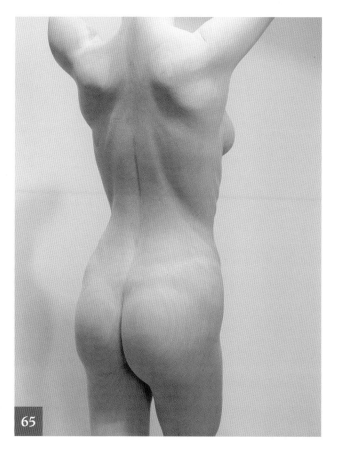

65

The carving is roughly sanded. The problem now is to make it into something desirable. To do that, compare the figure very carefully with the eight photographs of the live model and look for differences. Here's a list of what I found when I compared this photograph of the carving with the photograph of the model on page 95.

- The shoulder blade on the left of the picture is too lumpy.

- The narrow point of the waist on the left side is not at a sharp enough angle. The ribs should slope forward more, and the muscles running from the hips up the spine should be at a tighter angle.

- The profile of the buttock on the left should be flatter. The muscle should be tighter and the buttock narrower.

- The bottom line of the buttock should be higher and flatter.

- The buttock on the right should have a shallower curve.

- The area around the pelvis on the right-hand side should be less rotund and the narrow point of the waist lower and narrower.

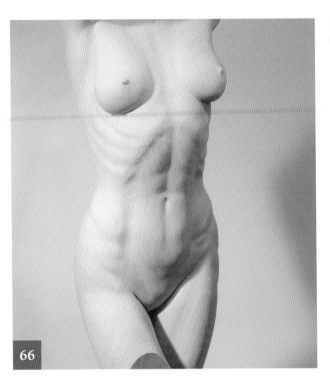

66

Looking to the front now, compare this photograph of the carving with the photograph of the model on page 92.

- Clearly, the left arm is in a different position to the original pose, but this can be discounted.

- On the right side, the hollow curve of the abdomen should be deeper and smoother. On the model, the curve then drops in quite a smooth line to the leg.

- The curve of the ribs on the left side of the stomach should be smoother.

- The buttock is too bulbous and should move down in a smooth, unbroken curve from waist to the thigh.

- The top of the left thigh on the inside edge should terminate in a shallow curve.

- The central groove above and below the navel needs to be more marked than I have it, and the "bikini line" needs to be clearer.

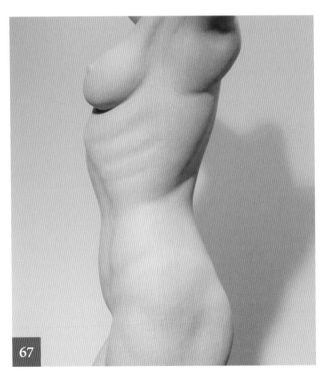

67

I now decided to depart from reality. I felt the ribs needed to be drastically reduced in prominence, so I sanded them down quite brutally. I then put in the navel and the two small depressions in the lower back. (See Step 70.) These depressions can be seen on one or two of the photographs of the model (pages 92 and 95).

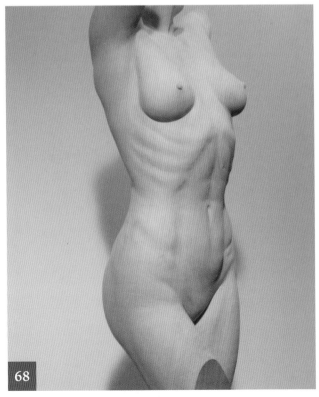

68

The revised carving from another view.

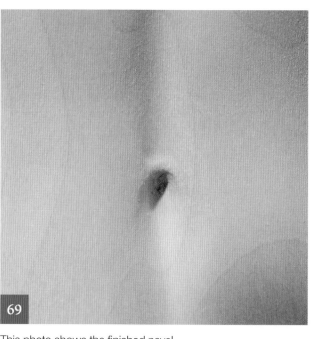

69

This photo shows the finished navel.

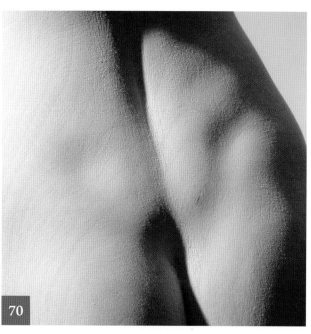

70

Here you can see the modeling on the lower back.

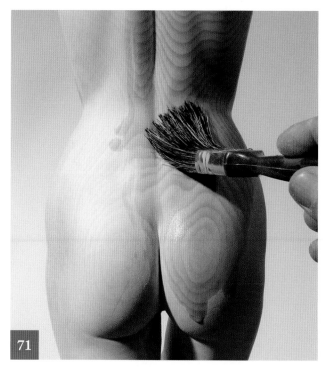

71

Continue sanding up to 240 grit. In sharp corners use folded sandpaper. I have found garnet paper to be best for this purpose because the grit does not flake off when folded. After using the 120-grit paper, wash the carving over boiling water. This raises the grain and brings out any deep scratches, dents or creases. When the carving is completely dry, continue with the sanding.

72

When the sanding is completed, cut away the bandsawed ends of the limbs. I prefer a kind of broken look, but a perfectly flat surface square across the limb is quite common in sculpture.

Sculpting the Female Face & Figure in Wood **117**

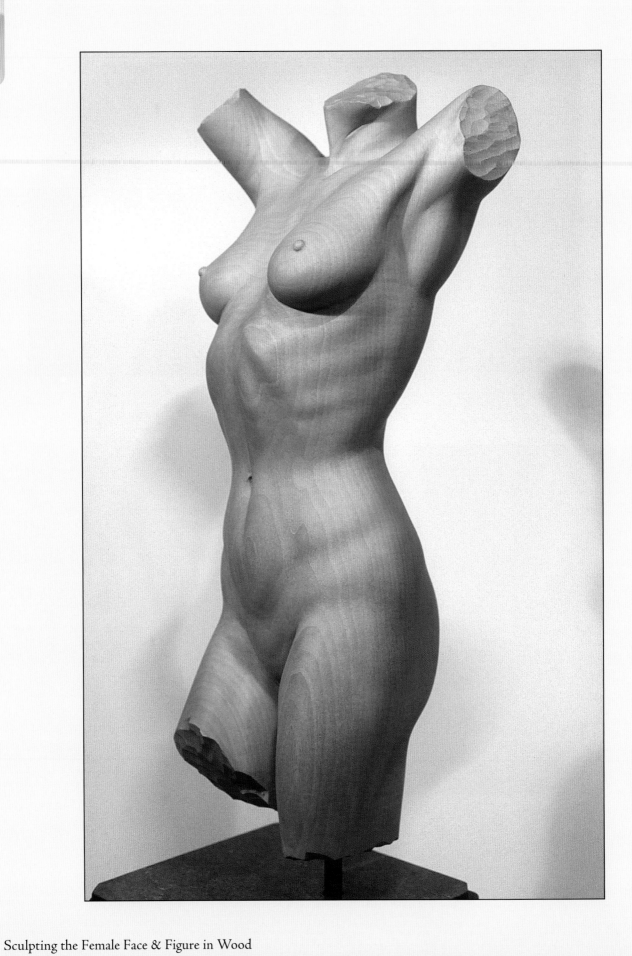

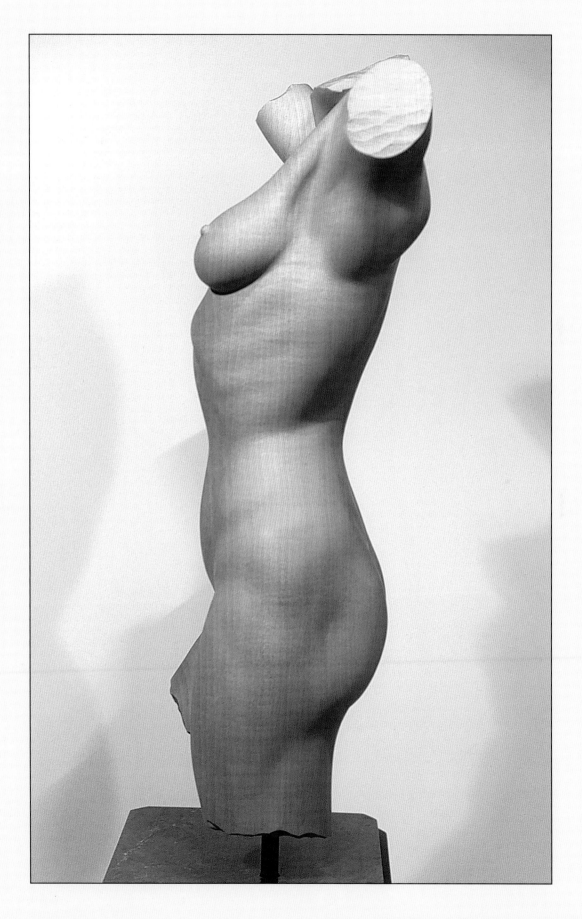

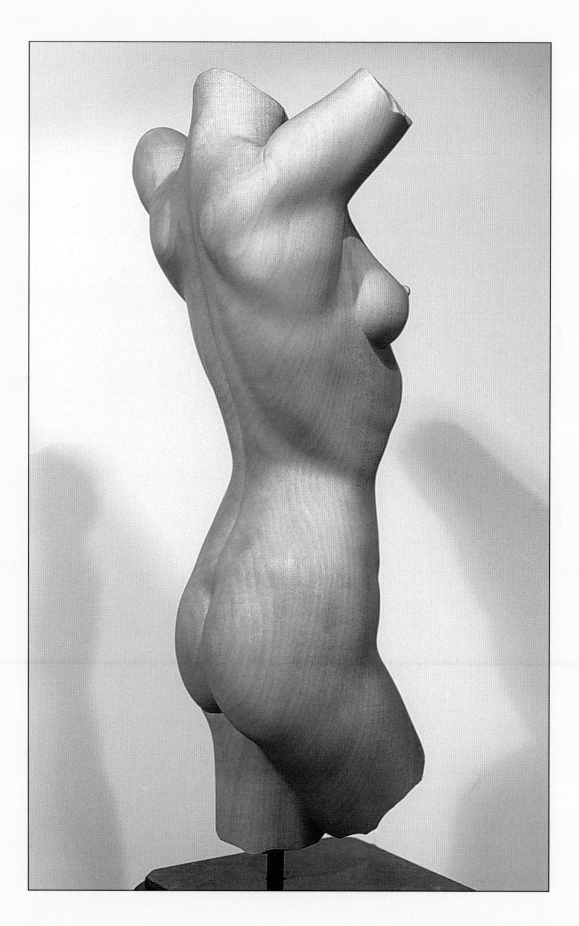

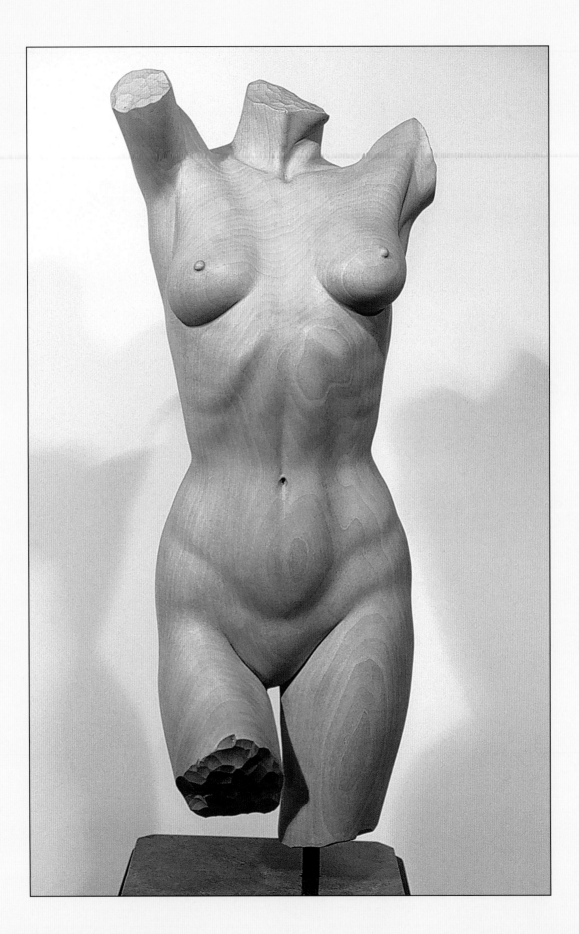

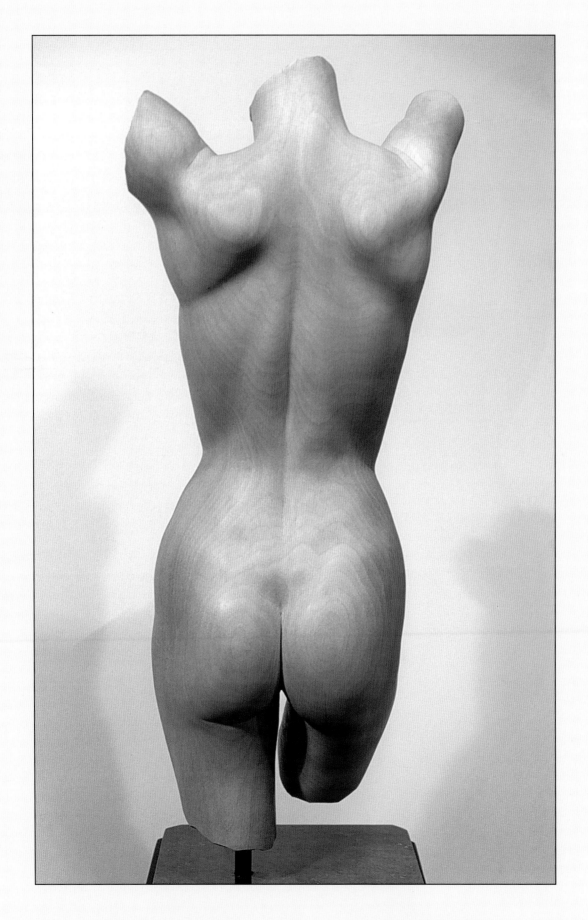

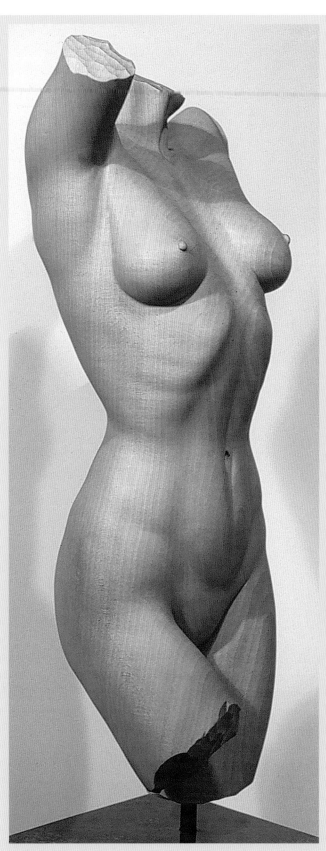

A Perfect Polish

When you are satisfied with the sanded surface (I usually use 80, 120, 180, 240 and 320 grits in progression.), the carving will need some kind of finish to enhance the wood and to protect it. Wood finishing is a huge subject, and theories and methods abound. Basically, you have two choices: Either employ a professional to do it for you or use a simple method yourself.

For years I used sanding sealer, followed by a wax polish. On simpler shapes, such as this torso, this kind of finish looks and feels very good. However, it is difficult to apply a wax finish on complex and fragile carvings; fine details can get clogged with wax. A wax finish also needs maintenance, which means that the person who owns the carving has to wax it now and then. Some people overdo it, and the piece ends up very shiny. Others neglect it, and the piece ends up dull and dusty. The fragile pieces often get broken.

The method I now use is to brush on a polyurethane varnish, not too sticky, and then immediately wipe it off with kitchen towels—and I mean really wipe it, as if you were getting a dirty mark off of the wood. In corners, wipe the varnish off with a dry brush. This leaves a very thin layer, with no brush marks, runs or puddles, that dries so quickly it does not get dusty. When the varnish is dry, repeat the process three or four times. I use a matte varnish, which gives a satiny finish, is waterproof and durable and never needs to be touched again.

CHAPTER 7

Carving a Torso in Walnut

The first project in this book was a very straightforward pose designed to give you an easy introduction to the female form. This second project is a far more energetic pose. To carve this piece requires good photographs, good working drawings and an ability to grasp three-dimensional shapes. The third item is something you will learn as you carve this and other female figures.

I decided to use walnut for this figure because its beautiful color and grain will add to the movement and vibrancy of the finished piece. Also this torso is very small, and I find it very pleasing to use the more valuable and exotic woods, which are usually only available in small dimensions on these small scale projects. The timber itself gives the piece a quality that would not be present if limewood were used.

10" high

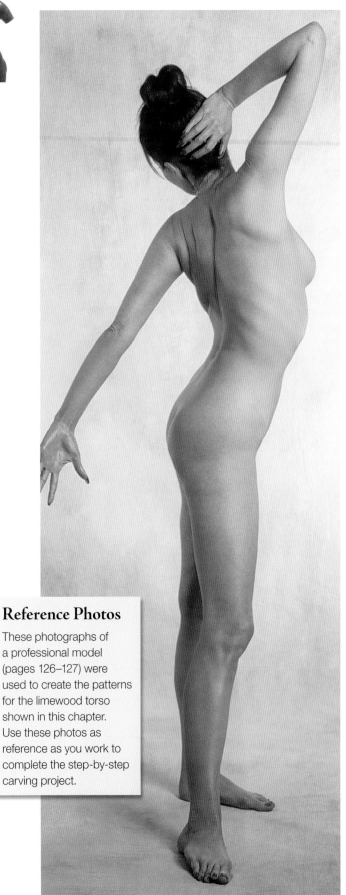

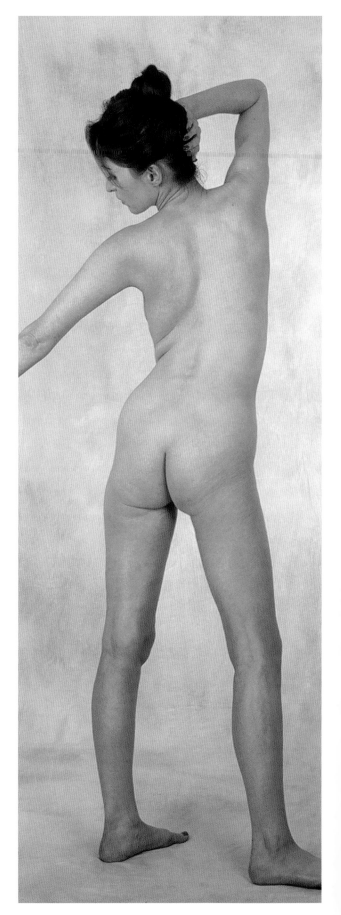

Reference Photos

These photographs of a professional model (pages 126–127) were used to create the patterns for the limewood torso shown in this chapter. Use these photos as reference as you work to complete the step-by-step carving project.

Sculpting the Female Face & Figure in Wood   **127**

WALNUT TORSO

Right side view   **Front view**

©IAN NORBURY

Use the front and side views shown here to bandsaw the blank. Cut very carefully, precisely on the line. Remember that tracing the plans onto a block of wood and bandsawing them allows for considerable accumulative errors. Only by taking great care can you reduce these errors to a minimum.

WALNUT TORSO

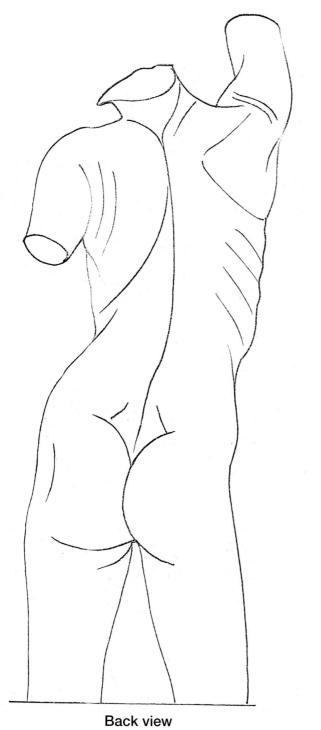

Back view

Left side view

The back and opposite side views are provided to show carving details.

1

All the preparatory work is done in exactly the same way as the first project. Here the bandsawed block (11" x 4" x 4") is ready to have the waste removed in front of the right shoulder. Cut this as a curved corner, not as a square cut. (See Step 6.)

2

Cut away the waste wood extending from the right arm across the back and the small block in line with the neck.

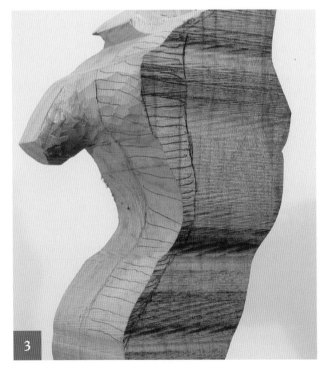

3

Remove the waste wood at the back. Note the curve where it meets the arm. This is not a square corner. Mark the line of the spine on the back and on the side. This area can be cut away to a square corner.

4

The right-hand side of the back has been reduced. The corner remaining between the arm and the back can now be carved in a curve where the shoulder is pulled back.

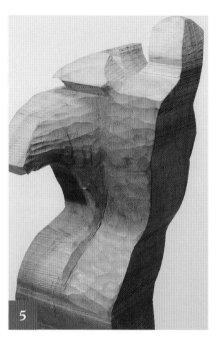

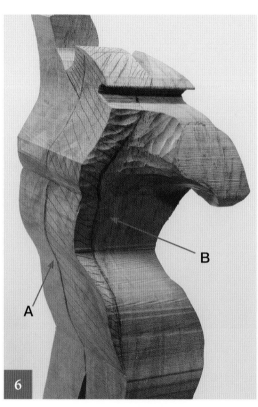

Draw the centerline on the front (A). On the right side draw the line running from the front of the neck, down the right side of the chest and ribs, and down to the bottom of the stomach (B). Cut this area into a corner. The block of waste in front of the neck can be cut away across to the left shoulder.

Cut the corner into a curve. Now return to the front of the figure.

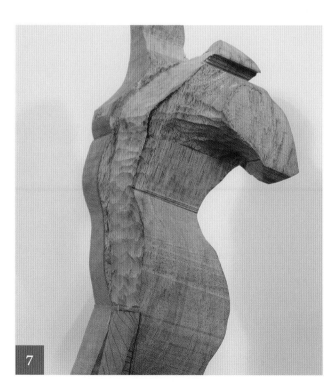

Cut back the right side of the front. These processes may seem strange and drastic, but it is the best way to achieve a positive twist to the body. Measure and cut to size the front of the right leg and the rear of the left leg.

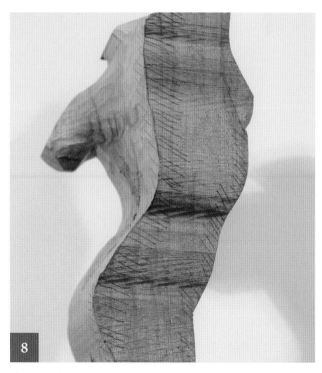

Having reduced the major areas of waste, you can now round off the corners. I did most of this with a round Surform rasp.

Sculpting the Female Face & Figure in Wood **131**

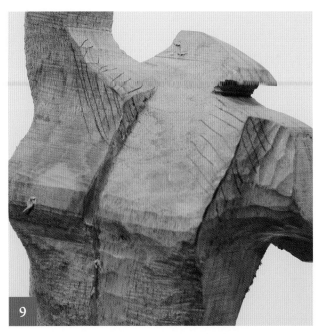

Shape the corner between the left arm and the neck into a curve where the muscle is pulled upward. Slope the right shoulder where it is pulled back by the arm.

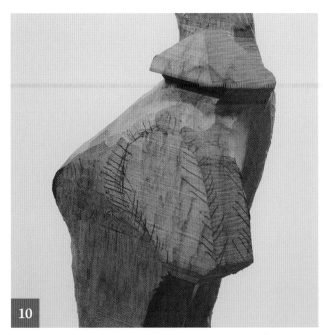

Round the right arm and shoulder.

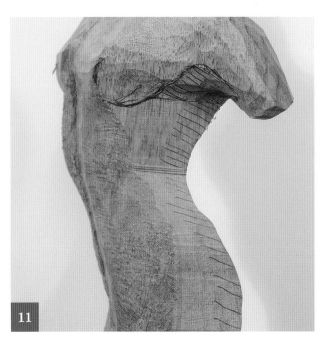

Locate the side view of the right breast and armpit. Cut into the armpit, and then round off the corner of the body.

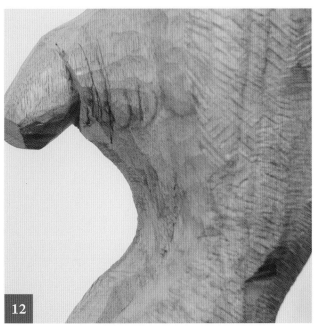

Moving to the back, cut in the deep folds behind the right shoulder and establish the dimension of the upper arm.

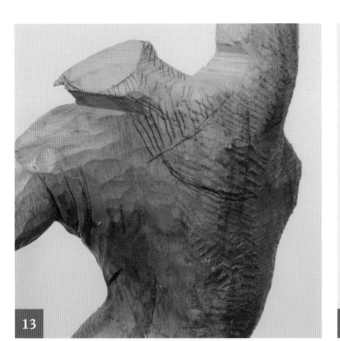

13

Round the neck and blend it into the back of the left shoulder.

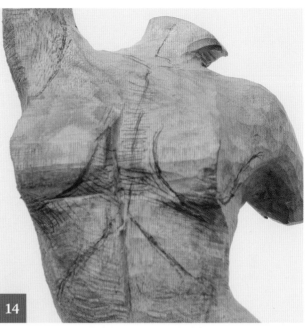

14

Mark the approximate lines of the breasts and the ribs. Cut away the waste between the breasts and round them off. Lightly cut in the lines of the ribs.

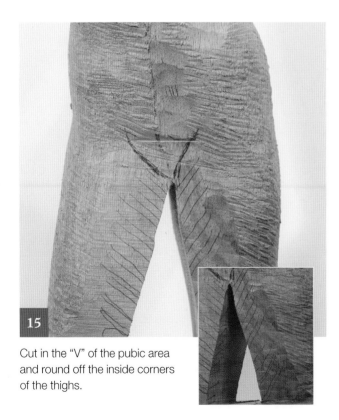

15

Cut in the "V" of the pubic area and round off the inside corners of the thighs.

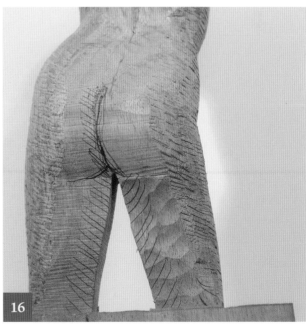

16

Cut in the division of the buttocks and round off the inside rear corners of the thighs.

17

The basic form of the figure should now be roughly established. Clean up the surface using files.

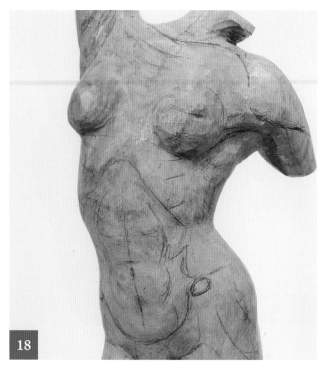

18

Using the anatomical diagrams and relating them to the photographs of the model, draw the main features onto the figure.

19

Cut these features in with gouges. By using this diagrammatic method, you have a positive system for establishing the physical features, even though they may not correspond to the particular model.

20

Repeat the same process on the back.

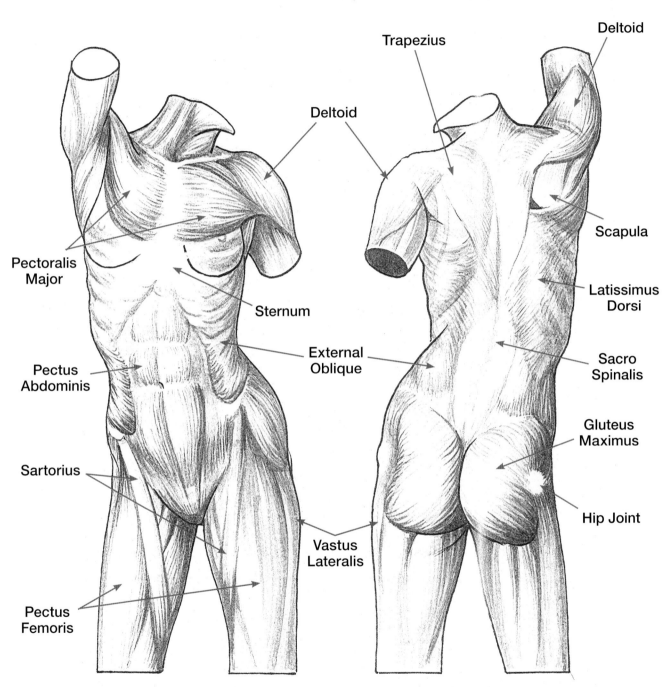

Trapezius

Deltoid

Deltoid

Pectoralis
Major

Scapula

Sternum

Latissimus
Dorsi

Pectus
Abdominis

External
Oblique

Sacro
Spinalis

Gluteus
Maximus

Sartorius

Hip Joint

Vastus
Lateralis

Pectus
Femoris

Diagram H: These anatomical sketches show the major muscle groups that come into play on a carving in this pose. Use these drawings in combination with the photographs to identify the cuts that will define this carving.

Sculpting the Female Face & Figure in Wood   135

CARVING A TORSO IN WALNUT

21

Rough sand the entire figure with 80-grit sandpaper.

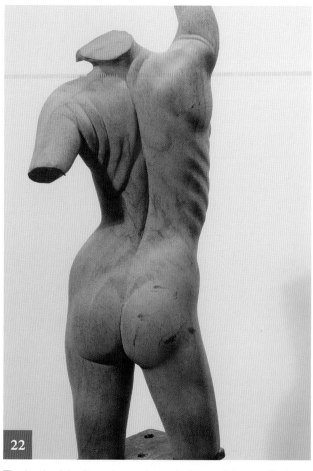

22

The back of the figure is rough sanded as well. In your final review of the project, look for discrepancies in the shapes of the ribs and pelvis, which are rigid and do not alter, regardless of movement.

Views of the finished piece from above and below show the dynamic twists in this torso. It is important to look down from the top of the figure, as well as across from the side, as you carve to ensure that the twist of the body is not resulting in deformities.

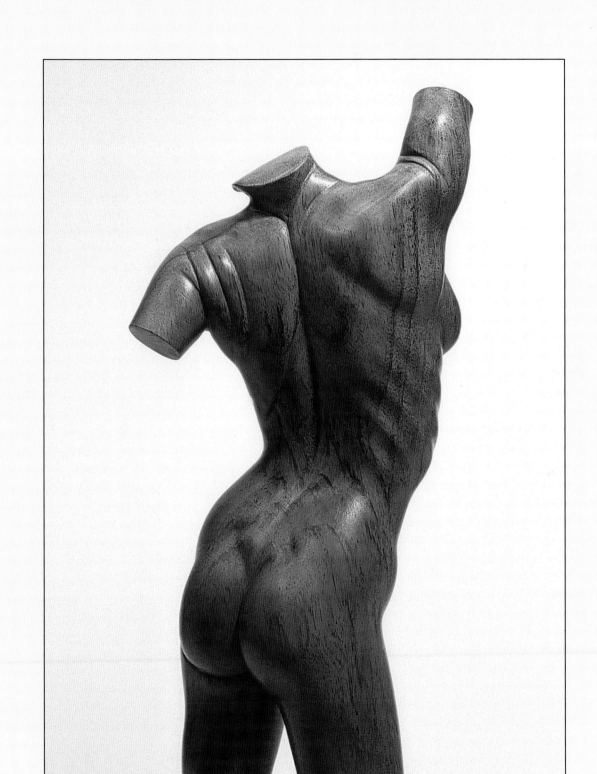

Index

More Great Books from Fox Chapel Publishing

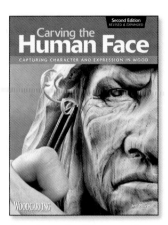

Carving the Human Face
ISBN 978-1-56523-424-6 **$24.95**

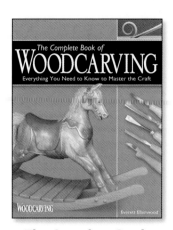

**The Complete Book
of Woodcarving**
ISBN 978-1-56523-292-1 **$27.95**

Carving the Female Face
ISBN 978-1-56523-145-0 **$12.95**

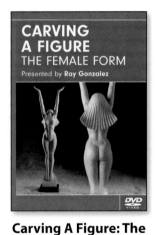

**Carving A Figure: The
Female Form — DVD**
ISBN 978-1-56523-413-0 **$24.95**

Carving Faces Workbook
ISBN 978-1-56523-585-4 **$19.95**

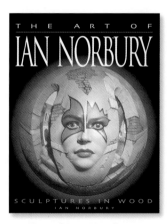

Art of Ian Norbury
ISBN 978-1-56523-222-8 **$24.95**

WOODCARVING
ILLUSTRATED

In addition to being a leading source of woodworking books and DVDs, Fox Chapel also publishes *Woodcarving Illustrated*. Released quarterly, it delivers premium projects, expert tips and techniques from today's finest carvers, and in-depth information about the latest tools, equipment, and materials.

Subscribe Today!
Woodcarving Illustrated: 888-506-6630
www.FoxChapelPublishing.com